The Christian and Government

by
John MacArthur, Jr.

MOODY PRESS

CHICAGO

© 1986 by
JOHN MACARTHUR, JR.

All Scripture quotations, unless noted otherwise, are from the *New Scofield Reference Bible*, King James Version. Copyright © 1967 by Oxford University Press, Inc. Reprinted by permission.

ISBN: 0-8024-5095-4

1 2 3 4 5 6 7 Printing/GB/Year 91 90 89 88 87 86

Printed in the United States of America

Contents

These Bible studies are taken from messages delivered by Pastor-Teacher John MacArthur, Jr., at Grace Community Church in Panorama City, California. The recorded messages themselves may be purchased as a series or individually. Please request the current price list by writing to:

WORD OF GRACE COMMUNICATIONS
P.O. Box 4000
Panorama City, CA 91412

Or call the following toll-free number:
1-800-55-GRACE

1

The Christian's Responsibility to Government—Part 1

Outline

Introduction
A. The Christian Perspective
  1. The inadequate responses
    a) In the past
    b) In the present
      (1) The assumed right
      (2) The attending result
        (a) The priority of the church
        (b) The priority of Scripture
  2. The important calling
    a) Christ's situation
      (1) A world of slavery
      (2) A world of absolute rulers
      (3) A world of high taxes
      (4) A world of persecution
    b) Christ's solution
  3. The inevitable conclusion
B. The Historical Background
  1. The rebellion of the Jews
    a) The Roman domination
    b) The scriptural defense
    c) The zealous defenders
  2. The reaction toward Christians
    a) The Roman reaction
      (1) Tolerance
      (2) Watchfulness
    b) The apostles' reminder
      (1) Paul
      (2) Peter

Lesson

I. The Principle (v. 1a)
   A. The Definitions
   B. The Duty
      1. The responsibility
         a) 1 Timothy 2:1-3
         b) Titus 3:1-2
      2. The limitation
         a) The example of Peter and John
            (1) The first persecution
                (a) The fearful restriction
                (b) The faithful response
                (c) The fruitful result
            (2) The second persecution

Introduction

Romans 13:1-7 says, "Let every soul be subject unto the higher powers. For there is no power but of God; the powers that be are ordained of God. Whosoever, therefore, resisteth the power, resisteth the ordinance of God; and they that resist shall receive to themselves judgment. For rulers are not a terror to good works, but to the evil. Wilt thou, then, not be afraid of the power? Do that which is good, and thou shalt have praise of the same; for he is the minister of God to thee for good. But if thou do that which is evil, be afraid; for he beareth not the sword in vain; for he is the minister of God, an avenger to execute wrath upon him that doeth evil. Wherefore, ye must needs be subject, not only for wrath but also for conscience sake. For, for this cause pay ye tribute also; for they are God's ministers, attending continually upon this very thing. Render, therefore, to all their dues: tribute to whom tribute is due; custom to whom custom; fear to whom fear; honor to whom honor." Those seven verses outline in brief and pointed terms the Christian's responsibility to government. This is the most clear and direct passage in all the New Testament on this subject. As a result, it is an extremely important passage for us to understand.

   A. The Christian Perspective

   The issue of the Christian's relationship to government has been vitally important throughout the history of the church. Christians always have been faced with a struggle in this matter because the church has found itself under all kinds of governments and rulers with different perspectives of leadership.

2

Traditionally and historically, the church in the United States has had less trouble with its response to government than the church has in many other countries—like our brothers and sisters who live in China, the Soviet Union, or countries behind the Iron Curtain. Since we live in a society that has been somewhat influenced by Christianity, we have had the benefit of the most benevolent of governments. But our circumstances are nothing like those of the Christians who lived in the days when the New Testament was being written, such as the believers in Rome who received Paul's letter.

1. The inadequate responses

In their struggle to answer the question of their relationship to government, Christians have not always answered it properly. Throughout the history of the church, people have decided that the right thing to do was revolt against the government in power and demand their rights—all in the name of Christianity. Wars were even begun for the same reason. Sometimes Christians have understood what their role is. But sometimes they have not understood their God-given role and have revolted instead of submitting. Laws have been violated in the name of Christianity.

a) In the past

In America, certain violations of law, civil disobedience, and subversive attempts to overthrow the powers on a local, state, or national level have been led by people who claimed to be Christians. Some Christians have decided that since they received bad treatment from certain governments, they were justified in their war against those governments.

To some people, evangelical Christianity was a proper justification for the American Revolution. They believed we had every right to kill Englishmen for the sake of our religious freedom. Some Christians I know personally refuse to pay their taxes because they believe that their freedoms are being violated. The truth is, the United States was born out of a violation of Romans 13:1-7 in the name of Christian freedom. That doesn't mean God won't overrule such violations and bring about good (which He did in this case), but the end never justifies the means.

3

b) In the present

Today we struggle over the issue of how we should identify with our government. Even though America once had a Christian orientation, we are now living in an era we could call post-Christian America. We are fortunate to often have presidents who affirm Christian faith and hold to Christian standards of ethics and morality, but our government in general no longer upholds the Bible as the source of truth and morality. We are seeing the erosion of such beliefs in our country.

(1) The assumed right

Since America seems to be losing its Christian orientation, there are some who believe Christians have a right to protest and break the law. Many Christian leaders are calling for Christians to leave their present ministry and become a part of a new political Christian lobby that uses pressure and social action to effect change. Some call for protest and moderate revolution against our government. They say the government is taking freedom away from the church and encroaching on religion. In an effort to save the church's freedom, myriads of organizations are rising up in our country, calling for action against the government. I am amazed at how many evangelical Christians, who would have avoided such activity fifteen years ago, are now aggressively pursuing the political lobby approach. I'm also amazed at the number of belligerent people who join together on issues of civil authority and civil rights, yet who would never find any common ground on the issue of truth. You can find true believers, charlatans, frauds, and false prophets all united for the sake of "religious freedom," who believe that political lobbying will preserve the kingdom of God in America.

(2) The attending result

One of the worst fallouts of the new preoccupation with political issues is that ultimately the ministry of the church is prostituted. People are selling themselves for something short of what the church is called to do. It cannot afford to

4

become a flag-waving, protest voice for governmental change. That's not its calling. I am appalled to see that many pastors have turned from an emphasis on the gospel to an emphasis on politics—from an emphasis on teaching the Bible to an emphasis on coalitions that support particular kinds of legislation. Worst of all, their emphasis is based on the ridiculous premise that the growth and impact of Christianity is somehow related to governmental policy in America.

a) The priority of the church

C. S. Lewis reminded Christians that human beings live forever, while the state is only temporal and thus is reserved to comparative insignificance (*Mere Christianity* [New York: Macmillan, 1977], pp. 78-79). To spend your time altering the state when you could be offering people eternal salvation is to make a bad choice. To abandon the message that gives life to the eternal soul in favor of temporal change prostitutes the purpose of a believer's life. That would be like a heart surgeon abandoning his life-saving practice to become a makeup artist. The church needs to use all its power and resources to bring men and women to Jesus Christ. That's what God has called us to do.

b) The priority of Scripture

Other than instructing us to be model citizens, Scripture says nothing at all about Christians engaging in politics. It says nothing about Christians engaging in civil change. Those things are not our priority. But that doesn't mean we're not to be involved as citizens. For example, in the Old Testament, Israel was a priestly nation. It was God's design for Israel to bring men to Him. And it was the primary function of the priests to do just that. There were other people to take care of menial problems and social issues. But the heart of the nation was the priesthood. The priests could not abandon their role of bringing men and women to God. That was God's design, and it is the same for the church. I believe we are a kingdom of priests, not a kingdom of politicians. Our purpose in the world is to bring men to God. You say, "Don't you care about change?" Of course I do, but I also know that change comes from the inside, not the

5

outside. We must administrate the things of the kingdom of God.

2. The important calling

The Christian's role in government has nothing to do with politicizing the church. It has nothing to do with getting involved in things that are good but not of divine priority. There is no biblical mandate for us to spend our time, money, and energy in matters of civil government. We are to be the conscience of the nation through godly living and faithful preaching. We do not confront the nation through political pressure but through the Word of God. We are to preach against sin and the evils of our time.

a) Christ's situation

Jesus came into a very interesting world:

(1) A world of slavery

Slavery flourished in the Roman Empire. There were approximately three slaves to every free man.

(2) A world of absolute rulers

The world was dominated by absolute monarchs and rulers. At the end of the Roman republic, the Caesars took power and ruled with absolute authority. Although Julius Caesar was murdered in the Roman senate in 44 B.C., that only served to accelerate the centralization of power. The senate declared Augustus proconsul and tribune of Rome for life, and he wielded absolute power. He was the commander in chief of the military, he reigned over the senate, and he controlled all civil affairs.

Jesus came into a world dominated by slavery and by one-man rule—the absolute antithesis of democracy that we hold so dear. All the power of the state was in one man's hands. The same thing was true in Palestine, where Herod had been placed as a puppet king under Roman rule. Herod was an Edomite, not a Jew. He ruled with such great power that he had the authority to demand that every baby in a certain region be massacred (Matt. 2:16). No one could stay his

6

hand. He had absolute authority over life and death. He even murdered members of his family—his wife, his wife's mother, and three of his sons.

(3) A world of high taxes

When Jesus came into the world, taxes were exorbitant. Those who worked as tax collectors had sold themselves to Rome for money and then overcharged the people. For example, when Zacchaeus the tax collector was converted, he immediately said he would pay back everything he had extorted fourfold (Luke 19:8). That was typical of the extortion that existed. So the taxes were unjust. In fact, Caesar Augustus decreed that a census (a registration with a view to taxation) be taken of all people in the world (Luke 2:1).

(4) A world of persecution

When Jesus came into the world, His people had become chattel for the Romans. They were an underprivileged and oppressed minority. They had no voice in Roman government and had to pay heavy taxes to their Roman taskmasters.

b) Christ's solution

That's a description of the world Jesus entered. The people didn't have democracy, the opportunity to vote, and many of the freedoms we enjoy. But what did Jesus say? He said, "Render, therefore, unto Caesar the things which are Caesar's; and unto God, the things that are God's" (Matt. 22:21). He did not come with power and force to overthrow Roman tyranny. He did not seek social change. He did not attempt to eliminate slavery. He did not come with political or economic issues at stake. He did not come to bring a new government or to wave the flag of Judaism. Those things were not the concern of His life and ministry. His appeal was always to the hearts of individual men and women, not to their political freedom and rights under government. Jesus did not participate in civil rights or crusade to abolish injustice; He preached the gospel of salvation. Once a man's or woman's soul is right with God, it matters very little what the externals are. Jesus was not

7

interested in a new social order but in a new spiritual order—the church. And He mandated the church to carry on the same kind of ministry.

3. The inevitable conclusion

The problems in Jesus' day were far more severe than ours. Today people living on welfare may have cars, TVs, and modern conveniences. We have to look at the issue differently when we determine how a Christian should respond to his government. Throughout all the generations of the church, Christians have had to struggle with this issue. But we have to come to some conclusion about what we are called to do and be in this society. What is our priority? What right does the government have over us? What is our proper response to that right?

Admittedly we live in tension. Personally, I'm not primarily concerned about political, economic, social, and civil issues. I do have a reasonable concern about those things, but they don't occupy my mind. The souls of lost men and women occupy my mind. Do they occupy yours? I'm not as concerned that people be happy, wealthy, and healthy as I am that they be saved. I only have so much energy, and the church only has so much power and resources. So I struggle with the millions of dollars that come out of evangelical hands for the purpose of politics. We need to be concerned about the souls of the lost.

What is our responsibility to government? How do we respond to the tension of being preoccupied with the kingdom of God yet being a good citizen in this world? First, the answer is not found in politics. God has called us to do two things. The first is in Romans 13:1: "Let every soul be subject to the higher powers." The second is in Romans 13:6: "For this cause pay ye tribute." The apostle Paul says two things are required of you as a Christian: submitting to the government and paying your taxes. That's our duty. Beyond that you ought to be busy doing the things that are eternally valuable to the kingdom. That is not to say the other things aren't important; it's just that they pale in importance when compared with the work of the kingdom. Be subject to the government, and pay your taxes. That's what Jesus meant when He said, "Render to Caesar." What does Caesar want? Submission to the laws and payment of taxes.

B. The Historical Background

In Paul's day, the response to government was a critical issue.

1. The rebellion of the Jews

   a) The Roman domination

   The Jews were notoriously zealous for their own identity, nation, independence, and religion. As a result, they constantly rebelled against Roman control. And although the Roman domination for the most part was beneficent and easy to bear, the Jews did not like being under the yoke of anyone. In John 8:33 the Pharisees tell Jesus that they had never been in bondage to anyone. But that was a ridiculous statement since at that very time they were under Roman domination. Prior to that they had been under the domination of the Greeks, Medo-Persians, Babylonians, and Egyptians. So they had a short memory. Actually the Pharisees were indicating not that they were under domination externally but that they had never been dominated in their hearts.

   The Jews didn't like the tyranny they were under, even though they enjoyed exceptional privileges in the Roman Empire. The empire that advocated Caesar worship and required everyone to worship him as a god allowed the Jews the right to worship their own God. The Romans safeguarded the Sabbath day, the Sabbath laws, the dietary laws, and the prohibition of idols. They made a law allowing no one to come inside the walls of the city of Jerusalem with any image of Caesar because that violated the Jewish law regarding idols. When the Jews wanted to kill Gentiles who had entered the inner court of the Temple, the Romans upheld their right to do so because it was required by the religious law of the Jews. The Romans were very gracious, but the Jews continued to chafe under their authority. They hated Roman domination. They questioned its legitimacy and fought against it.

   b) The scriptural defense

   As the basis for their hatred of the Roman yoke, the Jews used Deuteronomy 17:15: "Thou shalt surely set him king over thee whom the Lord thy God shall choose: one from among thy brethren shalt thou set king over thee; thou mayest not set a foreigner over thee, who is not thy brother." They did not want to have a king who was not Jewish, and Herod, Caesar, and Pilate were not Jewish. So they used that passage as a defense for their attitude toward the government. But they had forgotten that they were no longer living under the terms of Deuteronomy. They had so violated God's covenant that they were under judgment.

c) The zealous defenders

Among the Jews was a group known as the Zealots. They believed there was no king but God and that no taxes should be paid to anyone but God. They defied the government in every way—they wouldn't submit, and they wouldn't pay taxes. Instead, they embarked on violent action. The Zealots became murderers and assassins. They were known as dagger bearers—fanatical nationalists sworn to terrorism. They had a great influence on the Jewish populace. When the Jews saw Jesus' power, they immediately wanted to make Him king. Why? Because they wanted the ultimate revolt. They wanted to defeat Rome.

2. The reaction toward Christians

a) The Roman reaction

Roman law continued to be somewhat favorable to Christianity throughout the life of the apostle Paul. Rome viewed Christianity as nothing more than an offshoot of Judaism—a type of Judaistic cult.

(1) Tolerance

An interesting incident took place in Acts 18:12-17. The Corinthian Jews accused Paul of propagating an illegal religion. The Romans didn't allow many religions to exist, but they had legalized Judaism. When Paul came preaching Christ, the Corinthian Jews wanted to get him in trouble with the Roman authorities. So they went before proconsul Gallio and accused Paul of preaching an illegal religion. But Gallio paid no attention to their accusation, which indicates that he thought Christianity was nothing more than a few Jews disputing with other Jews about some element of theology. It was the attitude that Christianity was an offshoot of Judaism that gave Paul freedom in the Roman Empire to continue to preach the gospel of Christ over the next ten years. However, Christianity is different from Judaism, thus in reality it was not a sanctioned religion.

(2) Watchfulness

Even though Rome tolerated Christianity, the Romans also knew it needed to be watched. They knew that the founder of Christianity was Jesus Christ. They believed He was killed because He claimed to be a king and offered Himself as a rival to Caesar. So they knew there was a potential for trouble within Christianity. Although they tolerated it, they also watched it carefully.

There is no doubt that some Christians posed a threat to Roman authorities. Some were thought to be subversive. In fact, in Acts 17:6-7 unbelieving Jews were saying, "These that have turned the world upside down are come here also . . . and these all do contrary to the decrees of Caesar, saying that there is another king, one Jesus." The belief that their founder was a rival king defined Christians throughout the Roman Empire. But in spite of that, there was genuine tolerance for Christianity.

b) The apostles' reminder

(1) Paul

Paul is careful in what he says in Romans 13:1-7 because he doesn't want to be misunderstood. It was possible that if Christians pushed too hard for their freedoms and didn't respond properly to the Roman government, they could have been in trouble. The best thing Christians could do was continue to live peaceably and honorably as citizens in their society. They were not to be associated with the Jewish mentality of insurrection and rebellion. Paul writes this chapter to remind believers of their duty as citizens—to establish exemplary conduct epitomized by Christ, the apostles, and the believers in the earliest days of

11

the church. Paul wanted to separate Christianity from insurrectionist Judaism. He wanted to affirm that Christians are to be good citizens. Good citizenship is a question not only of not committing crimes but also of honoring and respecting those in authority over us.

In Romans 13:1 Paul establishes this basic principle: Whatever the form and whoever the ruler, civil government should be obeyed and submitted to by Christians. The Christian has a duty to his nation, even if the ruler is a Nero or a Hitler.

(2) Peter

First Peter 2:12 says, "Having your behavior honest among the Gentiles, that, whereas they speak against you as evildoers, they may by your good works, which they shall behold, glorify God in the day of visitation." In other words, "They may speak evil of you, but let that be a lie." But how are you going to promote goodness in a society that wants to persecute you? Verses 13-15 say, "Submit yourselves to every ordinance of man for the Lord's sake, whether it be to the king, as supreme, or unto governors, as unto them that are sent by him for the punishment of evildoers [the police]. . . . For so is the will of God, that with well-doing you may put to silence the ignorance of foolish men." Foolish men look for something to criticize. Your lack of good citizenship and obedience to the civil authority will give them their reason. Verse 16 says not to use "your liberty for a cloak of maliciousness." So Peter told a persecuted group of believers to accept and obey their authorities.

A Testimony from the Soviet Union

Georgi Vins is a Christian who lived for many years in the Soviet Union. He met with our staff one day, and we asked him what it was like to live under tyranny and repression in a communist country. He told us that Christians can't pursue an education or a career. They have no say in the government and no freedoms to speak of. The question was then posed to him: How do you respond to that kind of government? He said, "We obey every law in our nation, whether it appears to us to be just or unjust,

> except when we are told that we cannot worship God or obey the Scripture. But if we are persecuted, put into prison, or killed, it will be a result of our faith in Jesus Christ, not because we violated some law in our nation."

In Romans 13:1-7 Paul says the same thing Peter did: We have a serious responsibility to live out our justification by faith. Our self-sacrifice to the Lord (Rom. 12:1-2) should make us model citizens of our nation. We should not be known as protesters—as those who criticize and demean people in authority. We should speak against sin, injustice, evil, and immorality fearlessly and without hesitation. But we should give honor to those who are in authority over us. That is the biblical pattern for every age, every nation, and every Christian—it has nothing to do with America alone.

Lesson

I. THE PRINCIPLE (v. 1a)

"Let every soul be subject unto the higher powers."

That's the principle. It's unqualified, unlimited, and unconditional.

A. The Definitions

The phrase translated "every soul" is a Hebraism for "every person." The emphasis is on every individual person. Each of us has a very precise duty. The verb translated "be subject" is an imperative. The Greek word is *hupotassō*, a military term meaning "to line up to take your orders." Every one of us should get in line to submit to those who are commanding us. Who does the commanding? The higher powers. The phrase literally means "The authorities who have authority over us." That is a double phrase in the Greek text, *exousiais huperexousais*. They are the supreme ruling power. They're called "rulers" in verse 3. The text makes no distinction between good rulers and bad rulers or fair laws and unfair laws. In fact, it was the obedience of Christians to unfair laws and unjust rulers in times of persecution during the early years of the Roman Empire that brought tolerance and eventually acceptance of Christianity within that empire.

B. The Duty

We are called to submit. For those of us living in America, submission isn't unusually difficult because the laws are just, for the most part. They rightly represent divine truth. But they are changing fast, and we are to submit. We have to live in post-Christian America, although the nation has never really been Christian. There aren't Christian nations—only Christian people. Although things are changing in America, we still have the same duty.

1. The responsibility

   a) 1 Timothy 2:1-3—"I exhort, therefore, that first of all, supplications, prayers, intercessions, and giving of thanks, be made for all men, for kings, and for all that are in authority, that we may lead a quiet and peaceable life in all godliness and honesty. For this is good and acceptable in the sight of God, our Savior." God wants us to live a life that is peaceable. We should make peace; we should not make trouble or protest. We should live quiet, peaceable lives in all godliness and honesty. We affect the society from the inside by changing the hearts of the people, not the structure of society.

   b) Titus 3:1-2—"Put them in mind to be subject to principalities and powers, to obey magistrates, to be ready to every good work, to speak evil of no man, to be no brawlers, but gentle, showing all meekness unto all men." It bothers me to see people—supposedly in the name of Christ—speak against the leaders of our nation, no matter if those leaders are adequate or inadequate, just or unjust, fair or unfair.

   The principle of submission is repeated throughout Scripture. We saw it in 1 Peter, 1 Timothy, Titus, and we see it in Romans. You say, "Do you mean we're to submit to everything without limitation?" No. There is one limitation.

2. The limitation

   a) The example of Peter and John

      (1) The first persecution

          Acts 4:13 says that when the Jewish leaders "saw the boldness of Peter and John, and perceived that they were unlearned and ignorant men, they marveled; and they took knowledge of them, that they had been with Jesus." It was evident that they had been with Jesus because they had seen

14

them with Him and now heard their message. So they convened a council.

(a) The fearful restriction

The result of the council is in verses 16-18: "What shall we do to these men? For that indeed a notable miracle hath been done by them is manifest to all those who dwell in Jerusalem; and we cannot deny it. But that it spread no further among the people, let us threaten them, that they speak henceforth to no man in this name. And they called them, and commanded them not to speak at all nor teach in the name of Jesus." Now that is the decision of the authority, even though it is the religious authority.

(b) The faithful response

Verse 19 says, "But Peter and John answered and said unto them, Whether it is right in the sight of God to hearken unto you more than unto God, judge ye." There is now a serious conflict. In the person of Jesus Christ, God told them to go "into all the world, and preach the gospel to every creature" (Mark 16:15). But the authorities said not to preach. So Peter in effect says, "You tell us whom we should obey: you or God?" The answer is obvious, isn't it?

The one time we have a right to disobey the government is when it commands us not to do something God has commanded us to do, or when it commands us to do something God has commanded us not to do. For example, if all the laws that are being enacted for the rights of homosexuals should demand that Grace Community Church hire homosexuals, that's when we would say, "We won't hire them because you have just told us to do something that God has forbidden us to do." That is an occasion when we have justification for disobedience. I hope that if we are faced with having to disobey, we will have opportunity to speak loudly and clearly about why we stand with the truth of God.

15

(c) The fruitful result

Do you know what happened to Peter and John? In verse 31 they were having a prayer meeting with the other believers, "and they were all filled with the Holy Spirit, and they spoke the word of God with boldness." That shows you whom they decided to obey. They weren't quiet at all.

(2) The second persecution

In Acts 5:28 the apostles are being told again to be quiet: "Did not we strictly command you that ye should not teach in this name? And, behold, ye have filled Jerusalem with your doctrine, and intend to bring this man's [Christ's] blood on us." The apostles were not quiet; they accelerated their efforts. And part of their message was to tell the Jewish leaders that they were responsible for killing the Messiah.

Peter and the apostles had opportunities to say, "We ought to obey God rather than men." The only time a Christian can violate his government is when he is asked to disobey God. That's what Georgi Vins was referring to when he said, "If we're imprisoned or lose our life, it will be a result of our commitment to obey the Word of God when the government tells us not to."

There is no such thing as a Christian government. Don't assume that Paul is writing the book of Romans with a Christian government in mind. Certainly the government in Rome wasn't Christian. The only Christian government that will ever exist will be the one in the millennial kingdom. Until then, all governments will be flawed.

The Status of Missions in America

I thank God for the privilege of living under one of the best of human governments. I believe God has given two hundred-plus years to the United States of America in this time of redemptive history for one specific purpose. For the last two hundred years, America has been the primary source of missionaries to the world. We have seen that era come to a great climax in our lifetime. But now a change is coming about. I see other countries taking the lead in sending out missionaries. For the most part,

16

American church money has financed world missions for the last two hundred years. But our time of doing so may be done. God may bring up a new people to send out those who will reach His world for Christ.

If our government changes its form, as governments often do, we are still called to submit and be model citizens. We are called not only to obey but to obey with a spirit of obedience. We are to give honor to those who are in authority over us so that evil might not be spoken about the name of Christ. If there are critics who are looking for ways to condemn Christians, please let them condemn us for our faith and not our political viewpoints.

Focusing on the Facts

1. Why has the church always been faced with a struggle to determine its proper relationship to government (see pp. 2-3)?
2. Name some of the improper responses Christians have had towards their governments (see pp. 3-4).
3. What reason do some people use as justification for the American Revolution (see p. 3)?
4. What is one of the worst fallouts of the new Christian preoccupation with political issues (see p. 4)?
5. Why should Christians be considered as a kingdom of priests instead of a kingdom of politicians (see pp. 5-6)?
6. What is God's calling for every Christian (see p. 6)?
7. Describe the kind of world Jesus came into (see pp. 6-7).
8. What are some of the things Jesus didn't do in the world? What was His main concern (see p. 7)?
9. According to Romans 13:1 and 6, what two things has God instructed Christians to do concerning their government (see p. 8)?
10. Why did the Jews constantly rebel against Roman domination (see p. 9)?
11. Describe some of the privileges that the Roman government extended to the Jewish people (see p. 9).
12. What Scripture did the Jews use as the basis for their hatred of Roman domination? Explain (see pp. 9-10).
13. What was Rome's perspective of Christianity? What did that attitude allow Paul to do (see pp. 10-11)?
14. What was Paul's purpose in writing Romans 13:1-7 (see pp. 11-12)?
15. What basic principle did Paul establish in Romans 13:1 (see p. 12)?
16. What does Paul mean by the phrase "be subject" (Rom. 13:1; see p. 13)?

17. List some Scripture verses that delineate the Christian's responsibility to his government. Explain them (see p. 14).
18. According to Acts 4:18, what was the decision of the Jewish leaders regarding the preaching of Peter and John? How did Peter and John respond to that decision in verse 19 (see p. 15)?
19. What is the criteria for determining when Christians are allowed to disobey the government (see p. 15)?

Pondering the Principles

1. Do you struggle with your proper relationship to the government? What is your definition of a quiet and peaceable life? Begin a study of the life of Christ. You may want to obtain a harmony of the gospels to help. Based on your study, how did Jesus exemplify a quiet and peaceable life? How many times did He speak out against the evils of society? Explain each one. Based on Christ's pattern, what should you be doing? Remember, be sure your attitude is one of glorifying God by making His truth known. Don't let your actions allow people to be confused about your motives.

2. Suppose the government you lived under suddenly denied you all the social and political freedoms you now enjoy. How would you respond? Look up the following verses: Romans 13:1; 1 Timothy 2:1-3; Titus 3:1-2; 1 Peter 2:12-17. Based on the instruction of Scripture, how should your response to the government that gives you freedom differ from the one that denies you freedom? Please be obedient to God's Word by being obedient to your government.

2
The Christian's Responsibility to Government—Part 2

Outline

Introduction
A. The Intention of Romans
B. The Impact of Justification
   1. 1 Peter 2:12-15
   2. 1 Timothy 2:1-4
      a) Pray for the authorities
         (1) Jeremiah 29:7
         (2) 2 Corinthians 10:4
      b) Radiate saving grace
   3. 1 Thessalonians 4:10-12

Review
I. The Principle
A. The Definitions
B. The Duty
   1. The responsibility
   2. The limitation
      a) The example of Peter and John

Lesson
      b) The example of Daniel
         (1) The predicaments
            (*a*) Dietary defilement
               i) The appeal
               ii) The approval
            (*b*) Prevented prayer
         (2) The pattern
            (*a*) Obey in the Spirit
            (*b*) Disobey only out of necessity
            (*c*) Attempt peaceful resolve
            (*d*) Be willing to suffer punishment

II. The Reasons (vv. 1b-5)
  A. Government Is Decreed by God (v. 1b)
    1. Power reflects the purpose of God
    2. Governmental power is ordained by God
      a) The questions
      b) The purpose
  B. Resistance to Government Is Rebellion Against God (v. 2a)
    1. The definitions
    2. The duty
  C. Resistance to Government Results in Punishment (v. 2b)
    1. The methods of punishment
      a) Restitution
      b) Corporeal punishment
      c) Capital punishment
    2. The objectives of punishment
    3. The expediency of punishment
  D. Government Serves to Restrain Evil (v. 3a)

Introduction

Christianity is a total life experience. It is not an addendum to life. It touches every element of life—our thoughts, words, deeds, and relationships. Nothing is left unaffected by the transformation that the Lord Jesus Christ brings about in a life. Christianity cannot be isolated from any part of life. A study of the New Testament will show that the Spirit of God is involved in the totality of the Christian experience. In Ephesians 5 and 6, every relationship is touched by the Spirit of God in the life of a believer. It discusses husbands, wives, parents, children, masters, and servants. Colossians 3 talks about the same thing. Every relationship is impacted by the power of Christ.

  A. The Intention of Romans

    In Romans 13:1 the apostle Paul says that our Christianity affects our relationships to those in authority over us—to government and its rulers on a local and national level. We are given some very strict and clear direction from the Spirit of God on how we are to relate to the government. In Romans, Paul tells us that since we have been justified by grace through faith, made right with God, made citizens of His heavenly kingdom, and are now controlled by His Holy Spirit and living under His lordship, every dimension of life is different. In Romans 12:1-2, as a result of our new relationship with God, we are told to present ourselves to Him as living sacrifices. Then beginning in verse 3, Paul talks about

20

our relationship to other believers. We are to minister to them, love them, and be kind to them. Our relationship to those who have needs is discussed in verse 13. We are to distribute to the necessity of saints and be hospitable. Then Paul talks about our relationship to those who reject and hate the gospel. We are to bless and not curse those who persecute us (v. 14). Verse 21 says that we are to repay evil with good. We are not to wreak vengeance on anyone (v. 19). Paul is saying in the book of Romans that all our relationships are impacted by our justification.

B. The Impact of Justification

Many people believe that the epistle to the Romans is a great treatise on the doctrine of salvation. May I suggest that his discourse on salvation is only a means to an end? If Paul wanted to focus on the matter of justification only, he would end the epistle in chapter 11. But he doesn't. He goes on to deal with the implications of the doctrines that are laid down in the first eleven chapters. It is essential for the Christian to understand that his relationship to his government and those who are in authority over him is dramatically influenced by his salvation. We are called to live as model citizens so that we may reach the world around us with the saving gospel of Jesus Christ.

1. 1 Peter 2:12-15

Peter said, "Having your behavior honest among the Gentiles, that, whereas they speak against you as evildoers, they may by your good works, which they shall behold, glorify God in the day of visitation." How can we get unbelievers to glorify God? Peter said, "Submit yourselves to every ordinance of man for the Lord's sake, whether it be to the king, as supreme, or unto governors, as unto them that are sent by him for the punishment of evildoers, and for the praise of them that do well. For so is the will of God, that with well-doing ye may put to silence the ignorance of foolish men" (vv. 13-15). How you behave under the authorities in your country or city will demonstrate the legitimacy of your faith in Christ to that society. That is why we are to submit to whoever is in authority over us.

2. 1 Timothy 2:1-4

The apostle Paul wrote to Timothy with instruction for the church. First Timothy 3:15 says, "[I want you to] know how thou oughtest to behave thyself in the house of God, which is the church." Here is the principle of behavior for the church: "I exhort, therefore, that first of all, supplications, prayers, intercessions, and giving of thanks, be made for all men, for kings, and for all that are in authority, that we may lead a quiet and peaceable life in all godliness and honesty. For this is good and acceptable in the sight of God, our Savior, who will have all men to be saved, and to come unto the knowledge of the truth" (1 Tim. 2:1-4). There are two essential points that come out of those verses.

a) Pray for the authorities

We are to pray and give thanks to God for kings and all those in authority so that we may lead a quiet and peaceable life in all godliness and honesty. If we want to live the kind of godly life that God wants us to live, we need to pray for those in authority over us. We will not affect our rulers by protest, disobedience, or revolution but by prayer. We need to come to God in prayer so that we may lead a life of integrity. That is God's will for us because men will come to know the Savior when they see His people living godly lives.

(1) Jeremiah 29:7—"Seek the peace of the city to which I have caused you to be carried away captives." God's message to the Jews in captivity in Babylon was to seek the peace of that place. They were prisoners, but they were to seek peace and pray to the Lord for the nation of Babylon. The instruction of 1 Timothy 2:1-4 was given by Jeremiah: If you want peace in a society so that you can enjoy and spread your faith, then pray for those in authority over you. That is God's design.

(2) 2 Corinthians 10:4—"The weapons of our warfare are not carnal, but mighty through God to the pulling down of strongholds." The most powerful weapon that we as believers have to pull down the strongholds of the enemy is prayer. Revolution has no place in the Christian life; prayer is the priority.

In the book *Toward a Biblical View of Civil Government*, Robert Culver says, "Churchmen whose Christian activism has taken mainly to placarding, marching,

22

protesting, and shouting might well observe the author of these verses first at prayer, then in counsel with his friends, and after that preaching in the homes and market places. When Paul came to be heard by the mighty, it was to defend his action as a preacher . . . of a way to heaven" ([Chicago: Moody, 1974], p. 262). In other words, when it comes to political changes and governmental issues, pray. If you're going to be thrown into prison, make sure you're there for preaching the gospel of Jesus Christ and not for political protest.

b) Radiate saving grace

The goal of praying for the government is to lead a quiet and peaceable life so that you will have opportunity to see men saved and come to the knowledge of the truth. We pray that God will allow us the privilege of living a peaceable, quiet life radiating the saving grace of Jesus Christ. A tranquil life is to be the distinctive mark of a Christian.

3. 1 Thessalonians 4:10-12

I grieve when I hear rhetoric of anger, violence, and revolution. Paul says, "We beseech you, brethren, that ye increase more and more [in love], and that ye study to be quiet, and to do your own business, and to work with your own hands, as we commanded you, that ye may walk honestly toward them that are outside, and that ye may have lack of nothing."

All we can expect from government is protection of life and property. If government does that, it serves God's intended purpose. Unfortunately, there are failures in those areas, even in American society. For example, because of the number of lawsuits the government tolerates, many innocent people have to make great sacrifices just to defend themselves. Maintaining innocence comes at a great cost. I also believe that the United States government fails in the protection of life when it allows millions upon millions of abortions.

In spite of those things, we must pray and live a peaceful life. We influence the world by godly living and bold, confrontive, forthright preaching of the saving gospel of Jesus Christ—not by political protest or efforts to overthrow the government. The gospel must be our message. Like the prophets Amos, Nahum, and Malachi, we have every right to confront the sins of our society from the viewpoint of the Word of God. But we should not engage in political acts of violence or revolution.

Review

I. THE PRINCIPLE (v. 1*a*; see pp. 13-17)

"Let every soul be subject unto the higher powers."

That is the bottom-line command given to Christians. It does not discuss the character or qualifications of the authority. It doesn't discuss whether the authority is good or bad, elected or appointed, a republic or a monarchy; it just says that we are to be subject.

A. The Definitions (see p. 13)

B. The Duty (see pp. 13-17)

    1. The responsibility (see p. 14)

In Matthew 23:2-3 our Lord speaks to people at the Temple and says, "The scribes and the Pharisees sit in Moses' seat. All, therefore, whatever they bid you observe, that observe and do." The scribes and Pharisees had a God-given place of authority. However, the Lord also said not to be like them because they were hypocrites. But their authority had been granted by God even though they were still perverse men.

I'm amazed that in spite of the clarity of this command, many people persist in disobeying it, not only in American society and culture but in others as well. Jesus never taught His people to storm the bastille, revolt against the king, kill unjust rulers, march on city hall, barricade an administration building on campus, lead a sit-in at the president's office, harass leaders, or violate the law. The form of government was never an issue. It doesn't matter if it's capitalistic or socialistic, a democracy or a monarchy. The issue is simple: We are supposed to reach the world. To do so we have to demonstrate a godly, virtuous, peaceable life that will be attractive to others. If we are to let our light shine in a perverse and wicked generation, it must be "the light of the knowledge of the glory of God in the face of Jesus Christ" (2 Cor. 4:6).

    2. The limitation

There is only one occasion tolerated in Scripture for

violating the command to obey the government: when it demands us to do what God has forbidden us to do, or demands us not to do what God has commanded us to do.

a) The example of Peter and John (see pp. 14-17)

Lesson

b) The example of Daniel

Daniel is a very clear and precise illustration of a man who refused to do what the king said because it would have been in violation of what God had commanded.

(1) The predicaments

    (*a*) Dietary defilement

In Daniel 1, Daniel had been taken captive into Babylon with other young princes of Israel. Their Hebrew names are in verse 6: Hananiah, Mishael, and Azariah. Verse 8 says, "Daniel purposed in his heart that he would not defile himself with the portion of the king's food, nor with the wine which he drank." Daniel was instructed by the Babylonian monarch to eat his food. But to do that would have violated what Daniel knew to be a law revealed by God. The Jews had very circumspect dietary laws, and Daniel would not defile himself with food that was not prescribed by God.

i) The appeal

Daniel's attitude was characterized by a spirit of submission. Verse 8 says that he "requested of the prince of the eunuchs that he might not defile himself." Daniel asked permission of the one who was over him and under the king. He asked for a test: "I'll commit myself to eating what I prefer to eat. After ten days you come back. We'll examine those who have eaten the king's food and compare them to me. I will eat just vegetables. Then we'll see who looks the best" (vv. 12-13). That was a conciliatory way for Daniel to seek to obey God without becoming abrasive to the man who was carrying out orders from his king.

ii) The approval

According to verse 14, the man consented to the test. When the ten days were ended, he checked everyone. Daniel and his friends surpassed all the others and rose to places of prominence. Daniel could have protested and been disrespectful to the one over him. He could have bad-mouthed the king. But he sought a conciliatory means to obey God without compromise in the midst of a difficult situation.

(b) Prevented prayer

In Daniel 6 is the familiar account of Daniel in the lions' den. The setting is now the Medo-Persian kingdom.

The Honor of Serving in Government

There is nothing wrong with serving in a civil, state, or federal government position. It is an honored position. Daniel is the best example of that truth in Scripture. Every time he avoided compromise, he received a greater reputation. As a result of his uncompromising spirit, he was constantly promoted until he became the prime minister of the Medo-Persian kingdom. It is an honor to serve in government, not a dishonor. But it was Daniel's conciliatory yet uncompromising attitude that caused him to prosper.

In Daniel 6:4-9 the princes of the kingdom wanted to get rid of Daniel, so they got the king to sign an edict that no one was to pray to anyone but the king. Of course, Daniel continued with his prayers because he knew that was right before God. For his obedience to God he was thrown into a den of lions. But Daniel was never disrespectful. Verse 21 says, "Then said Daniel unto the king, O king, live forever." That appears to be a strange thing for a man to say to the one who had thrown him into a den of lions, but Daniel understood that the powers that be

26

are ordained of God. He trusted that no matter what the king did, he was in the hands of God, who delivered him. Verse 28 says, "So this Daniel prospered in the reign of Darius, and in the reign of Cyrus, the Persian."

(2) The pattern

The uncompromising approach of Daniel and his friends meant disobeying the government. But Daniel's attitude serves as a model for all those who have to face the reality that you can't do what the government says when it conflicts with what God desires. Daniel and his friends Hananiah, Mishael, and Azariah never wavered from honoring the king or being respectful. Let me give you the pattern I see flowing out of the experience of Daniel.

(a) Obey in the Spirit

Normally, we are to obey, respect, and do everything we can to please those in authority. We are to be model citizens—obedient not only outwardly but also in spirit.

(b) Disobey only out of necessity

We resist and disobey only when we are commanded to do something the Word of God forbids or are forbidden to do something the Word of God commands. Those two occasions are illustrated in Daniel's prophecy. He would not do what the Word of God forbade—eat certain kinds of food. And he would not stop doing what God had commanded him to do—pray.

(c) Attempt peaceful resolve

When government and the Word of God conflict, we should not disobey until we have done all we can to try to resolve the conflict peacefully. Daniel went to his leader and said, "Isn't there something we can work out so I can maintain my convictions and you can carry on with your responsibilities?"

(d) Be willing to suffer punishment

> If disobedience is necessary, we must be willing to suffer the consequent punishment. If we are called to obedience and our government tells us we will be punished for disobedience, then we have to quietly and peacefully accept it, just as Daniel did when he went into the lions' den. We must commit ourselves to God's care.

We should always have a respectful and honorable attitude to our authorities. That kind of attitude speaks volumes about the integrity of the Christian faith. Christianity is not a political lobby or a social perspective limited to a particular concept of social or economic existence; it is a matter of the salvation of man's soul.

II. THE REASONS (vv. 1b-5)

We are to be subject to the powers that are over us. Why? Paul gives seven logical reasons.

A. Government Is Decreed by God (v. 1b)

"For there is no power but of God; the powers that be are ordained of God."

Any form of civil authority comes directly from God. Government is an institution, just like marriage. The relevancy of the institution does not depend on who the couple is, what their life-style is like, or what their level of commitment is, because marriage is instituted by God, not by man. The church is another institution of God. The makeup of the participants doesn't determine the relevancy of the institution, but the fact that God ordains it does.

1. Power reflects the purpose of God

> Paul says, "There is no power but of God." That means there is no power in existence that isn't reflective of the purpose, will, and authority of God. No civil government exists in any nation of the world apart from God. Psalm 62:11 says, "Power belongeth unto God." All power, all creation, all things in heaven and earth belong to God. The entire world belongs to Him. Man exists solely as a result of God's creative act and will. God created the world for His own purposes. He alone is sovereign. Anyone who possesses any sovereignty on earth has had it delegated to him by God.

28

2. Governmental power is ordained by God

All governmental authority is from God. You say, "Are you also referring to communist China and the Soviet Union?" Yes. All power that exists is ordained of God. There is not one power that is not reflective of a God-ordained authority. He is the ultimate Sovereign.

When the apostle Paul preaches on Mars Hill in Acts 17, he says this about the nations in verse 26: "[God] hath made of one blood all nations of men to dwell on all the face of the earth, and hath determined the times before appointed, and the bounds of their habitation." God is the One who designed and created nations. The gift of authority is a divine gift. No tyrant ever seized power without God allowing him to.

a) The questions

You are probably asking yourself some questions: What about the cruel governments? How can you say that about communist governments? How can you say that about Adolf Hitler? How can you say that about abusive governments? How can you say they are ordained of God? I didn't say it; the Bible did. There is no power but of God, and the power that exists is ordained by God.

What about cruel abuses in government? The injustices of government are not a reflection of God's holy nature and will. Although there is apostasy in the church, the institution itself is ordained of God, and the apostasy is no reflection of the nature of God. Abuses do not deny the sacredness or authority in any of God's institutions—be it the home, church, or government. To be honest, men abuse all God's gifts. Wicked rulers are part of God's plan to punish wicked nations and allow evil to run its course toward destruction.

b) The purpose

God has designed by His sovereign purpose a reason for every government that exists. Some exist for the benefit of people who have done well, some for the punishment of those who have done evil. We cannot second-guess God's purpose for instituting a certain kind of government in a certain place. He has ordained government to protect and preserve men—to protect their lives and their property. To do that, government has been given the role of repressing evil and honoring virtue.

Paul says, "The powers that be are ordained by God." They are not ordained by the will of the majority. The majority simply reflects the sovereign purpose of God. The powers that be are God's design. So the first reason for submitting to government is that it exists by the decree of God. Government is expressive of the divine will—sometimes He wants to punish a nation, sometimes He wants to prosper a nation. Sometimes He wants to bless a people, sometimes He chooses to judge a people. But government, in all its forms, is decreed by God.

B. Resistance to Government Is Rebellion Against God (v. 2*a*)

"Whosoever, therefore, resisteth the power, resisteth the ordinance of God."

If you resist your government, you are resisting an institution of God.

1. The definitions

The Greek word that is translated "ordinance" here is *diatagē*.

The word means "institute." The Greek word for "resisteth" is *antitassō* and is used here in the perfect tense. The verse could read, "Whoever has—and continues to have—a permanent attitude of resistance against the government is resisting God." In 1839 Robert Haldane in his commentary on Romans wrote, "The people of God, then, ought to consider resistance to the government under which they live as a very awful crime—even as resistance to God Himself" (*An Exposition of the Epistle to the Romans* [MacDill AFB, Florida: MacDonald, n.d.], p. 579).

2. The duty

It was of no consequence whether the Roman emperor was kind or good, a persecutor or lover of Christians, elected by the people or appointed by the senate. It was not important whether the assertion of imperial authority by Caesar was just or unjust, good or wicked. None of those things matter. Government, in whatever form it takes, exists for the purpose of God. That is why resis-

30

tance and rebellion against government are resistance and rebellion against God.

Unless it is obvious that the government has overstepped its bounds and is forcing us to do something that is contrary to all that Scripture indicates, we are to obey it. God operates in the maintenance of government. We are to honor that government, whether it is represented by the president, the governor, the senate, the house, or the police.

Do you remember David's horror when he had occasion to kill Saul (1 Sam. 24:7)? He wouldn't do it because he understood the truth of honoring the one in authority. The people of Israel were to teach their children that the penalty for being disobedient to one's parents was death. That impressed upon everyone the need to give honor to authority (Ex. 21:15, 17). Government is divinely decreed, and to resist it is to resist God.

C. Resistance to Government Results in Punishment (v. 2b)

"They that resist shall receive to themselves judgment."

If you resist the government, you're going to be punished. The Greek word *krima* means "judgment." It is used in 1 Corinthians 11:29 of the judgment of God. But it is used in Romans 13:2 primarily in reference to the punishment that God brings through civil authorities. God has ordained government to punish evildoers. If you resist the government, you will be punished. But if you are like Daniel and have to resist because you have a higher command from God's Word, then you accept the punishment. But if you choose to resist because you want to, you will deserve punishment.

1. The methods of punishment

A study of punishment in the Old Testament is fascinating. There were several methods.

a) Restitution

Our home was robbed recently. Some things of great value were taken, such as a gold watch that had been my grandfather's and some of the silver my wife and I received when we were married. The police called sometime later to tell us that they had caught the men who robbed us. Unfortunately, our items had been taken to a fence somewhere in Hollywood and had

31

been melted down and removed before the police could recover them. They went on to tell us that one of the criminals was released on bail, while the other one was being held because of an outstanding warrant for his arrest. Then they said, "We regret to say that there is no way you'll ever recover the goods that were taken." That made me think about the Old Testament pattern of restitution. A criminal wasn't punished by putting him away in a prison; he was given the dignity of paying off his debt to the nation by working with his hands. Ephesians 4:28 says, "Let him that stole steal no more but, rather, let him labor, working with his hands the thing which is good, that he may have to give to him that needeth." The implication is to restore a man's dignity so he can make restitution.

b) Corporeal punishment

Punishment was also physical. It was often executed by whippings so that pain came instantaneously, and shame was public. But then it was over, and the person went on with life. He had paid for his crime. If he committed another crime, he would be punished again.

c) Capital punishment

If the crime was worthy of death (there were some thirty-five different crimes that carried the death penalty), the person was quickly put to death.

The system of punishment in Israel was simple. For lesser crimes, there was corporeal punishment and restitution. For greater crimes, there was death.

2. The objectives of punishment

The objective in punishment was multiple. First, it was a matter of justice. Second, it was a deterrent to crime. Third, it was a restraint on criminals. Fourth, it allowed for rehabilitation—the penalty was paid, and the person continued with life. He wasn't put into prison with other criminals so he could learn how to be a better criminal. Immediate punishment also prevented private vengeance.

Are Prisons Biblical?

There were no prisons in Old Testament Judaism, and there is no indication from the text of the Old Testament that the Israelites were to operate prisons. They were a part of the Roman social order and other pagan societies.

In Jeremiah 37:15, Jeremiah is incarcerated in a home that was made into a prison. That indicates to me there was no official prison. Prisons are not endorsed biblically. Instantaneous payment of the penalty was exacted from all criminals. Severe punishment such as whippings were given. Then the opportunity to make restitution was also given, which restored the man's dignity.

In the early days of America, the Puritans used corporeal punishment. You may remember from your American history books the pictures of people sitting in stocks with their heads, hands, and arms stuck through holes. We say, "Oh, how painful! I can't imagine being that way for three or four days!" They used corporeal punishment because they understood it was scriptural. For severe crimes, the punishment could have been banishment or even execution.

The Quakers first introduced the prison system in America. The first American prison was called the "Walnut Street Jail." By 1790 the law had established imprisonment as the normal way to punish criminals.

There are a half million prisoners in the United States today. We have the highest crime rate in the Western world. Do prisons work? No. Prisons are breeding grounds for homosexuality and brutality. Crime schools operate within prisons. One writer calls the American prison system "unbiblical, inhumane, ineffective, inefficient, and idiotic." According to statistics released in 1982, we punish 25 out of every 500 criminals who commit serious crimes. The 25 that are punished are put someplace where they sit for years. Many people advocate the rights of prisoners. Some prisons are becoming country clubs, so much so that criminals often don't mind being there. They receive free meals and are cared for by the state.

3. The expediency of punishment

   In Old Testament economy, the government had the right to punish people immediately and physically. It enforced restitution, which allowed the criminal the opportunity to gain back his dignity and pay his debts.

The restitution process was usually conducted by assigning that criminal to a family. He lived with and was cared for by that family while he worked out his restitution. What a dignified way to restore a man's character!

Whatever the crime demanded, the punishment was to be given swiftly. Ecclesiastes 8:11 says, "Because sentence against an evil work is not executed speedily, therefore the heart of the sons of men is fully set in them to do evil." If a speedy sentence is not brought about, men will do evil. And sentencing for crimes is not performed speedily at all in American society.

Punishment of evildoers is a God-given right of the government. When a person violates the law, he should expect to be punished because God has given the state the right to do so. Human authority performs the punishment but only as representatives of God. The instruments of punishment are human, but the source of the laws is God.

The Breakdown of Government

When we forget that government is an institution of God and begin to allow evil to go unpunished, the entire government begins to break down. I fear that politicking isn't going to change that. I think we are watching the collapse of American government and society. There's only one way to change that, and it's not by political action. The saving gospel of Jesus Christ is to be our priority.

We are to submit to the government because it is from God. To rebel against it is to rebel against God, and to resist it brings punishment.

D. Government Serves to Restrain Evil (v. 3a)

"For rulers are not a terror to good works, but to the evil."

Did you know that even a communist Chinese or Soviet government restrains evil? All the governments behind the Iron Curtain restrain evil. There is no government on the face of the earth that will punish you for failure to rape someone, rob someone, or murder someone. Even the worst kind of governments deal rightly with matters of right and wrong.

I was talking with someone from Ethiopia not long ago who told me that Ethiopia's government is in unbelievable turmoil. We would say that would be the worst kind of government. I asked this individual what the crime situation was like in Ethiopia. I was told that three years ago there was a rape in Addis Ababa (the capital of Ethiopia and a city of a million people), but there hasn't been one since because the rapist was hanging in the marketplace the next day. Now, you might not like the politics and style of the government in Ethiopia, but like any government it is in the business of at least knowing the difference between right and wrong.

The knowledge of good and evil is a product of the Fall. When Adam and Eve ate of the tree of the knowledge of good and evil, they learned about good and evil. Even fallen, sinful people know about good and evil. I don't like to say this, but you would be safer on the streets of Iran at night than you would be on the streets of Los Angeles. If you committed a crime in Iran, you wouldn't last very long. They at least know what crime is, and they deal with it. But that doesn't mean, however, that we would want to live under that kind of a government.

Government serves to restrain evil. Even those governments that we wouldn't want to identify with or be subject to have some understanding of right and wrong.

Focusing on the Facts

1. What does Romans 12 say about the result of a Christian's relationship to God (see pp. 20-21)?
2. Why are Christians called to be model citizens (see p. 21)?
3. Why do Christians need to live godly lives (1 Tim. 2:1-4; see p. 22)?
4. What should you do if you want peace in your society (see p. 22)?
5. How can Christians best influence the world (see p. 23)?
6. When Daniel had been commanded to eat the king's food, how was he able to remain obedient to God without being abrasive to the authorities (Dan. 1:12-13; see pp. 25-26)?
7. How did Daniel treat the king after he had thrown Daniel into a den of lions (Dan. 6:21; see pp. 26-27)?
8. Describe the pattern that Daniel sets for all Christians (see pp. 27-28).
9. Explain what Paul meant by saying, "There is no power but of God" (Rom. 13:1; see p. 28).
10. Does God ordain communist governments? Explain your answer (see p. 29).
11. Why is resistance to government resistance against God (see p. 30)?
12. What happens to those who resist the government (Rom. 13:2; see p. 31)?

13. Explain the methods of punishment in the Old Testament (see pp. 31-32).
14. What were the objectives in the Old Testament methods of punishment (see p. 32)?
15. What happens when crimes are not punished swiftly (Eccles. 8:11; see p. 34)?

Pondering the Principles

1. Read 1 Timothy 2:1-4. Do you pray for your governmental authorities at all, a little, or a lot? Do you pray for all the authorities over you, or do you just concentrate on the leader of your country? Set aside part of your prayer time to pray for your authorities, including your senators and representatives in both the federal and state government. Pray for your governor, mayor, and other elected officials in your city. Pray for your police department. You may even want to contact their offices to find out some of the specifics you could pray for. As you are faithful to pray, you will be fulfilling one of God's designs for your life.

2. When the government institutes a law that you disagree with, how do you respond? How should you respond if the law does not cause you to disobey God? What is to be your attitude in obeying your government? If you find yourself constantly questioning governmental decisions, perhaps you need to examine your attitude. Ask God to show you how your attitude to your government is lacking. Ask Him to convict you of those times when your attitude isn't what it should be. Finally, remember that a positive attitude to your government will reflect your obedience to God.

3
The Christian's Responsibility
to Government—Part 3

Outline

Introduction

Review
I. The Principle (v. 1a)
II. The Reasons (vv. 1b-5)
  A. The Government Is Decreed by God (v. 1b)
  B. Resistance to Government Is Rebellion Against God (v. 2a)
  C. Resistance to Government Results in Punishment (v. 2b)

Lesson
  D. Government Serves to Restrain Evil (v. 3a)
    1. The principle defined
      a) Understanding basic morality
        (1) Genesis 2:15-17
        (2) Romans 2:14-15
      b) Preserving life and property
    2. The principle fulfilled
      a) It acts without pity
      b) It acts without partiality
      c) It acts without delay
    3. The principle tested
      a) Paul's unfavorable treatment
      b) Paul's favorable treatment
  E. Government Serves to Promote Good (vv. 3b-4a)
    1. The citizens: receiving praise (v. 3b)
    2. The government: serving God (v. 4a)
  F. Government Has the Right to Punish with Death (v. 4b)
    1. Instituting the penalty
      a) Genesis 9:6
      b) Matthew 26:52
      c) Acts 25:11

2. Inflicting the penalty
   a) The avenging government
   b) The bloodguilty government
3. Interpreting the penalty
G. Submission to Government Builds the Conscience (v. 5)

Introduction

The familiar portions of the epistle to the Romans are about salvation. The great argument of Romans runs from chapter 1 to the end of chapter 11. In it, Paul lays out the doctrines of justification and sanctification. Beginning in chapter 12 Paul gives the practical applications of those doctrines. Since we've been saved and set apart to God, we are to commit ourselves to a certain kind of living. Within the range of that life is a proper relationship to government—to the authority under which a Christian lives. In Romans 13:1-7 Paul tells the Christian that he has two responsibilities: to be subject to the government and pay taxes.

Review

I. THE PRINCIPLE (v. 1*a*; see pp. 13-17, 24-28)

II. THE REASONS (vv. 1*b*-5)

Paul gives seven reasons for being subject to the government. And this subjection is unqualified; it is not determined by the kind of government, the benevolence of the government, or the theology of the government. Our subjection is simply a matter of obedience to the plan of God. He has ordained governmental authority for the protection of life and property.

A. Government Is Decreed by God (v. 1*b*; see pp. 28-30)

B. Resistance to Government Is Rebellion Against God (v. 2*a*; see pp. 30-31)

C. Resistance to Government Results in Punishment (v. 2*b*; see pp. 31-34)

Lesson

D. Government Serves to Restrain Evil (v. 3*a*; see pp. 34-35)

"For rulers are not a terror to good works, but to the evil."

38

Government is designed to put fear in the hearts of people who do evil but not to those who do good. Verse 3 continues, "Wilt thou, then, not be afraid of the power? Do that which is good, and thou shalt have praise of the same." Closely connected to the idea of punishment is the idea of fearing the government if you do evil.

1.   The principle defined

The word "fear" is *phobos* in the Greek text. We get the word *phobia* from it. It refers to certain terror. Paul is saying that government is not a terror to people who do good works. The phrase "good works" refers to a class of deeds that are inherently good. But the government is a terror to those who do evil works—a class of deeds that are inherently evil. The government moves against people in society who perform evil deeds—who break the law. And that is why they have reason for having a certain amount of terror. Rulers are to bring terror to those who do evil. A government—if it is doing its job—must put fear in the hearts of evildoers. That is a basic function of government. You and I are well aware of what happens in a government that doesn't put fear into the hearts of evildoers. The results are tragic.

a)   Understanding basic morality

In general, secular rulers know the difference between good and evil. Let me show you why.

(1)   Genesis 2:15-17—"The Lord God took the man, and put him into the garden of Eden to till it and to keep it. And the Lord God commanded the man, saying, Of every tree of the garden thou mayest freely eat; but of the tree of the knowledge of good and evil, thou shalt not eat of it; for in the day that thou eatest thereof thou shalt surely die." What did Adam and Eve do? They disobeyed God and ate from the tree of the knowledge of good and evil. Therefore, when Adam and Eve sinned, they gained a knowledge of good and evil. That knowledge has been passed down through all the sons and daughters of Adam. Every man and woman that enters this world has an inherent knowledge of good and evil.

(2)   Romans 2:14-15—"When the Gentiles, who have not the law [the written law], do by nature the things contained in the law, these, having not the

39

law, are a law unto themselves; who show the work of the law written in their hearts." People of the unregenerate world have the law of God written in their hearts. What does that mean? The knowledge of good and evil is a part of everyone's conscience. In theological terms, that is referred to as "natural revelation" as opposed to "special revelation," which is Scripture.

The government of man knows the difference between good and evil. Even pagans understand basic morality through human reason, natural revelation, and common grace.

b) Preserving life and property

Even the most evil society or the worst government will hold to a basic preservation of life and property. Unfortunately, some good governments do very poorly at it, while some evil dictators do very well. Even the poorest government is a blessing compared to no government at all. Can you imagine what would happen in a society with no one in control? It would instantly self-destruct. If people had only themselves to protect their lives or property, there would be constant war.

God has built into the heart of man a sense of what is right and wrong in very basic terms. So government is put in place by God for the purpose of preserving life and protecting property. It then becomes a terror to those who do evil—those who steal property or take lives. But it is not a terror to those who do good. Government is designed to create this fear by taking swift action against those who do evil.

2. The principle fulfilled

Let me give you some insight into how a government is to act if it fulfills its God-ordained role to the maximum.

a) It acts without pity

In Deuteronomy 19:13 we learn that a government is to act against evildoers without pity. A murderer is in view here: "Thine eye shall not pity him, but thou shalt put away the guilt of innocent blood from Israel, that it may go well with thee." In other words, "If you don't do to a murderer what he has done to someone else, you can be sure you will not prosper."

40

That's God's promise. A government is to act against an evildoer without pity. Verse 21 says, "And thine eye shall not pity, but life shall go for life, eye for eye, tooth for tooth, hand for hand, foot for foot." There is to be equal retribution without pity. Why? Verse 20 says, "Those who remain shall hear, and fear, and shall henceforth commit no more any such evil among you." If you do not exact punishment without pity, then people won't have the fear that will restrain them from doing evil.

b) It acts without partiality

No one should be set apart because of personal preference. Deuteronomy 13:6-10 says, "If thy brother, the son of thy mother, or thy son, or thy daughter, or the wife of thy bosom, or thy friend who is as thine own soul, entice thee secretly, saying, Let us go and serve other gods, which thou hast not known, thou, nor thy fathers, namely, of the gods of the people who are round about you, near unto thee, or far off from thee, from the one end of the earth even unto the other end of the earth, thou shalt not consent unto him, nor hearken unto him; neither shall thine eye pity him, neither shalt thou spare, neither shalt thou conceal him. But thou shalt surely kill him; thine hand shall be first upon him to put him to death, and afterwards the hand of all the people. And thou shalt stone him with stones, that he die, because he hath sought to thrust thee away from the Lord thy God, who brought thee out of the land of Egypt, from the house of bondage."

The principle detailed in those verses was unique to Israel because it was a theocracy, and the crime was leading people to worship a false god. But the point I want you to see is that there is no restriction of who could be put to death. It didn't matter if the disobedient person was one's brother, son, wife, or friend; there is no partiality in fulfilling the law of God. Then verse 11 says, "All Israel shall hear, and fear, and shall do no more any such wickedness as this is among you." If government began acting without pity and partiality when executing justice, it would go a long way in convincing evildoers to change their ways.

41

c) It acts without delay

Deuteronomy 25:2-3 says, "And it shall be, if the wicked man be worthy to be beaten, that the judge shall cause him to lie down, and to be beaten before his face, according to his fault, by a certain number. Forty stripes he may give him, and not exceed." When the judge finds a man guilty, he gives him what retribution is due right on the spot. Punishment needs to be immediate so it is obvious to all that judgment is swift.

If government acted without pity, partiality, and delay, it would be a terror to evildoers. Unfortunately, we have seen the erosion of that principle. We often hear the cry of pity for the criminal. I understand the need for mercy, but I also understand what happens when mercy becomes the norm, and everyone thinks he can do what he wishes and escape judgment. We are well aware that certain people seem to receive partial treatment for what they have done, whereas others are more severely punished. And we all know that punishment in America is anything but without delay. If the government acts as it should, it will deter the criminal and put fear in the hearts of evildoers.

We are to submit to God's ordination of government. It is from Him. To rebel against it is to resist God. To resist Him is to bring punishment upon yourself. Government is designed to restrain evil. As Christians, we don't want to tear down what God has put in place to uphold goodness and restrain evil.

3. The principle tested

What happens if the government treats you badly? What should you do if it takes away your freedoms and encroaches on you in ways that you feel are unfair, unjust, or inequitable? Look at the example set by the apostle Paul.

a) Paul's unfavorable treatment

Paul and his companion Silas were put in jail in Philippi even though they didn't do anything to deserve it. The accusation takes place in Acts 16:20-24: "These men, being Jews, exceedingly trouble our city, and teach customs which are not lawful for us to receive, neither to observe, being Romans.

42

And the multitude rose up together against them; and the magistrates tore off their clothes, and commanded to beat them. And when they had laid many stripes upon them, they cast them into prison, charging the jailer to keep them safely . . . and [make] their feet fast in the stocks." But what were Paul and Silas doing at midnight? Singing praises (Acts 16:25)!

It is true that Paul and Silas were treated unfairly, yet it was Paul who said that we're to submit to the government. He knew what it was like to endure injustice: He was beaten with rods three times and stoned once (2 Cor. 11:25). We also need to remember that Jesus Christ suffered unjustly, yet He upholds the principle. The truth stands in spite of those times when government oversteps its bounds.

b) Paul's favorable treatment

Paul had a different experience in Acts 19:35-41: "When the town clerk had quieted the people, he said, Ye men of Ephesus, what man is there that knoweth not that the city of the Ephesians is a worshiper of the great goddess, Diana, and of the image which fell down from Jupiter? Seeing, then, that these things cannot be spoken against, ye ought to be quiet, and do nothing rashly. For ye have brought here these men, who are neither robbers of temples, nor yet blasphemers of your goddess. Wherefore, if Demetrius, and the craftsmen who are with him, have a matter against any man, the law is open, and there are deputies; let them accuse one another. But if ye inquire anything concerning other matters, it shall be determined in a lawful assembly. For we are in danger to be called in question for this day's uproar, there being no cause for which we may give an account of this concourse. And when he had thus spoken, he dismissed the assembly."

In Acts 16 we see an occasion where government acted against the apostle Paul. In Acts 19 we see it act in his defense and rescue him from a mob. We should not obviate the principle of obeying the government. There are times when government may overstep its bounds, and there are times when we may depend on its provision. In either case, we need to be submissive.

43

E. Government Serves to Promote Good (vv. 3b-4a)

1. The citizens: receiving praise (v. 3b)

"Wilt thou, then, not be afraid of the power? Do that which is good, and thou shalt have praise of the same."

Our government has been ordained to bring praise to those who do good. Paul is saying, "Do what is good, and you won't have to fear because you will have praise from those in authority." If you enjoy a quiet and peaceful life—a life of goodness—and if you demonstrate the love of Christ, godliness, and virtue rather than making trouble, you will find yourself receiving praise.

2. The government: serving God (v. 4a)

"For he is the minister of God to thee for good."

Government becomes the servant (Gk., *diakonos*, "deacon") of God by doing good to you. The ruler's purpose is not only to be a terror to those who do evil, but also to offer praise to those who do good. Rulers have been granted great honor because they are servants of God. The president of the United States is a servant of God. The senators, assemblymen, and justices of the United States all the way down to the officials in state and city governments are all servants of God. They carry out a God-ordained service. They uphold a divine institution. They may not know God personally, but they represent him and His desire for peace and safety among men.

We are to do all we can to keep peace, live honorably with dignity, cultivate harmony, and be model citizens so that those who serve God in government may honor us. Evangelical, fundamental Christians who truly hold up the name of Christ should be the model of what a citizen should be in society. That will enable those who are the servants of God in government to see in them something unique and attractive.

Robert Haldane in his commentary on Romans said, "The institution of civil government is a dispensation of mercy, and its existence is so indispensable, that the moment it ceases under one form it re-establishes itself in another" (*An Exposition of the Epistle to the Romans* [MacDill AFB, Florida: MacDonald, n.d.], p. 581). When a coup takes place in a country, it will never eliminate government; it will only result in the exchange of government because man cannot survive without it. Haldane goes on to say, "The world, ever since the fall, when the dominion of one part of the human race

44

over another was immediately introduced . . . has been in such a state of corruption and depravity, that without the powerful obstacle presented by civil government to the selfish and malignant passions of men, it would be better to live among the beasts of the forest than in human society. As soon as its restraints are removed, man shows himself in his real character. When there was no king in Israel . . . every man did that which was right in his own eyes" (p. 581).

We are called to submission because God is the source of government. To rebel against government is to resist God, and to resist God brings judgment because government serves to restrain evil and promote good. We should desire to be good so that we might enjoy the benefits of government.

F. Government Has the Right to Punish with Death (v. 4b)

"But if thou do that which is evil, be afraid; for he beareth not the sword in vain; for he is the minister of God, an avenger to execute wrath upon him that doeth evil."

If you do what is evil, be afraid, because God has given the government the right to bear the sword—and it doesn't bear the sword for nothing. You don't spank or fine people with a sword; you kill people with a sword. So Paul is saying that government is given the right to inflict final punishment—the punishment of death. God has ordained civil government to bear the sword for the purpose of putting evildoers to death. If you have ever wondered if capital punishment is biblical, you have your answer in this verse. The sword is a symbol for death.

1. Instituting the penalty

a) Genesis 9:6—When God was laying down some basic matters regarding human government, He said, "Whoso sheddeth man's blood, by man shall his blood be shed; for in the image of God made he man." Man is sacred because he was made in the image of God. If someone took the life of a man, that person was to forfeit his own life. And government should execute that penalty without pity, partiality, or delay.

b) Matthew 26:52—Peter took out his sword and started to attack the soldiers who were coming to arrest Jesus. Then the Lord said, "Put up again thy sword into its place; for all they that take the sword shall perish with the sword." He was telling Peter that if

45

he took a life, he would die because that was the law. The Lord is upholding capital punishment. If you fight with the sword, you will die by the sword. That is a divine institution.

c) Acts 25:11—Paul said this to Festus the governor: "If I be an offender, or have committed anything worthy of death, I refuse not to die." Why did Paul say that? Because he knew that is God's standard. He affirmed the right of government to take his life if he had violated a law and was deserving of death.

The Old Testament prescribes the death penalty for murder, striking one's parent, blasphemy, witchcraft, involvement in the occult, false prophecy, rape, immorality, homosexuality, kidnapping, idolatry, and a blasphemous violation of the holiness of the Sabbath. God has ordained government to have the right to take a life.

2. Inflicting the penalty

Romans 13:4 says that the government is the minister of God. Part of the ministry of God in government for the good of man is to make evildoers afraid of the sword. Government is to serve God as an avenger of those who have been wronged. God requires capital punishment for those who commit crimes deserving that penalty. Robert Culver says, "What must not be lost sight of is that unpleasant as is the task of the jailor and the use of the whip, the cell, the noose, the guillotine, these things stand behind the stability of civilized society, and they stand there necessarily, for God has declared it so, in harmony with reality, rather than with apostate sociological opinion. Government, with its coercive powers is a social necessity, but one determined by the Creator, not by the statistical tables of some university social research staff! No society can successfully vote fines, imprisonment, corporeal and capital punishment away permanently. The society that tries has lost touch with realities of man (his fallen sinful state), realities of the world, and the truth of divine revelation in nature, man's conscience, and the Bible" (*Toward a Biblical View of Civil Government* [Chicago: Moody, 1974], p. 256). Society can't do that and survive. God has ordained government to bear the sword.

46

a) The avenging government

Vengeance belongs to God, and it often comes through the government. Romans 12:19 says, "Dearly beloved, avenge not yourselves but, rather, give place unto wrath; for it is written, Vengeance is mine; I will repay, saith the Lord." As Christians, we can thank God that government has the right to use the sword. I don't like to think of people losing their lives, but I think the way to stop people from murdering each other is to make it very clear that if you take a life, you'll immediately lose yours. That will protect the sanctity of life.

b) The bloodguilty government

When deaths are not satisfied, a nation becomes bloodguilty.

(1) Genesis 4:9-11—Cain murdered Abel. Verse 9 says, "The Lord said unto Cain, Where is Abel, thy brother? And he said, I know not: am I my brother's keeper?" He was not only a murderer but a liar as well. Satan is the father of lies and has been a murderer from the beginning (John 8:44). So Cain was mirroring the one who had no doubt inspired him to kill Abel. The Lord said, "What hast thou done? The voice of thy brother's blood crieth unto me from the ground. And now art thou cursed from the earth, which hath opened her mouth to receive thy brother's blood from thy hand" (vv. 10-11). When Cain killed Abel, his blood cried out to God because it was unrequited. A life had been taken with no life given in return. There had been no retribution.

In Genesis 9:6 God lays down the following principle: "Whoso sheddeth man's blood, by man shall his blood be shed." A murderer is to lose his life. That alone will satisfy the unrequited blood and in turn satisfy God.

(2) Genesis 42:22—"Reuben answered them, saying, Spoke I not unto you, saying, Do not sin against the child; and ye would not hear? Therefore, behold, also his blood is required." Joseph's brothers had sold him into slavery, and now they were feeling guilty for doing so. Reuben told them that until a life was given for Joseph's life,

47

God would remain unsatisfied. He recognized the principle that God had established.

(3) Joshua 2:19—Spies from Israel told Rahab, who had helped them escape, "And it shall be, that whosoever shall go out of the doors of thy house into the street, his blood shall be upon his head, and we will be guiltless; and whosoever shall be with thee in the house, his blood shall be on our head, if any hand be upon him." Whenever there was guilt from the loss of a life, someone's blood had to be shed. That is why the men told Rahab, "His blood shall be on our head, if any hand be upon him."

(4) 2 Samuel 4:11—This chapter describes the murder of Ish-Bosheth, Saul's son. Verse 11 says, "How much more, when wicked men have slain a righteous person in his own house upon his bed? Shall I not, therefore, now require his blood of your hand, and take you away from the earth?" If you take a life, you give a life. Your blood is required for his blood. The pattern is the same throughout the Old Testament. Blood was required for the shedding of blood.

(5) Ezekiel 7:20-27—"As for the beauty of his ornament, he set it in majesty; but they made the images of their abominations and of their detestable things of it; therefore have I set it far from them. And I will give it into the hands of the strangers for a prey, and to the wicked of the earth for a spoil, and they shall pollute it" (vv. 20-21). When the Babylonians invaded Jerusalem, they profaned the Temple. The Lord continued, "My face will I turn also from them, and they shall pollute my secret place; for the robbers shall enter into it, and defile it. Make a chain; for the land is full of bloody crimes" (vv. 22-23). The primary reason that God brought judgment on Israel during the Babylonian captivity was that the nation was full of bloody crimes—murders for which there had been no retribution. The blood was crying out to God, and the city was full of violence. If you show me a place where the rulers don't execute murderers

and those who commit severe crimes, I'll show you a place full of violence.

The Lord continues, "Wherefore, I will bring the worst of the nations, and they shall possess their houses; I will also make the pomp of the strong to cease, and their holy places shall be defiled. Destruction cometh; and they shall seek peace, and there shall be none. Mischief shall come upon mischief, and rumor shall be upon rumor; then shall they seek a vision from the prophet, but the law shall perish from the priest, and counsel from the ancients. The king shall mourn, and the prince shall be clothed with desolation, and the hands of the people of the land shall be troubled; I will do unto them after their way, and according to their deserts will I judge them; and they shall know that I am the Lord" (vv. 24-27). God is saying, "I'm going to bring terrible judgment because this land is full of bloody crimes and violence, since judgment is not executed on evildoers."

(6) Ezekiel 18:10-13—After describing what a man will receive if he is obedient, God describes what will happen if the man's son is disobedient: "If he beget a son that is a robber, a shedder of blood, and that doeth the like to any one of these things, and that doeth not any of those duties, but even hath eaten upon the mountains, and defiled his neighbor's wife, hath oppressed the poor and needy, hath spoiled by violence, hath not restored the pledge, and hath lifted up his eyes to the idols, hath committed abomination, hath given forth upon interest, and hath taken increase, shall he then live? He shall not live; he hath done all these abominations; he shall surely die; his blood shall be upon him." Bloodguiltiness must be requited. Those kinds of crimes must be paid for with blood.

3. Interpreting the penalty

Does God do that because He hates people? No. God knows that when capital punishment is executed properly, it becomes a terror to evildoers and restrains them from doing evil. Men need restraints because they are

49

basically vile. God requires the death penalty not that He can kill people but that people will not have to die. When the law of the land is made according to the law of God, it restrains the criminal. Then there will be no victims or perpetrators. But when blood is shed and it remains unrequited, the nation becomes guilty, and God will judge it.

Numbers 35:33 says, "So ye shall not pollute the land wherein ye are; for blood defileth the land: and the land cannot be cleansed of the blood that is shed therein, but by the blood of him that shed it." The land will never be cleansed of shed blood until that blood is requited.

Why Is America in Such a Mess?

I could suggest many reasons for the predicament that America is in. For one, this nation is under the judgment of God for unrequited blood, which cries out to Him for retribution against murderers, robbers, and others who are worthy of death. Were they dealt with properly, the number of victims and perpetrators would be minimized. But they are not, and our land is guilty. I believe with all my heart that abortion is murder. Our nation is guilty to an inconceivable extent in this massacre of unborn children.

Pacifism is not advocated in the New Testament. Government has the right to the sword. If it doesn't use it, the land cries out for unrequited blood. This land cries out for the blood of millions upon millions of unborn children who were murdered. It also cries out for all the other unsatisfied murders. Most of the killers have never been made to face retribution. I believe that is reason enough for God to bring judgment against the United States even as He did against Israel. It has become full of bloody crimes—a land filled with violence.

G. Submission to Government Builds the Conscience (v. 5)

"Wherefore, ye must needs be subject, not only for wrath but also for conscience sake."

You need to be subject not only because you fear the consequences but also because you know what is right. Your motivation isn't all negative, and right should be the highest motivation. Yet fear has to be a factor. There needs to be punishment without pity, partiality, or delay. There must be blood for blood, an eye for an eye, a tooth for a tooth, a hand for a hand, and a foot for a foot. Yes, we are to conform because we fear. But the higher motive is to conform not only for wrath's sake but also for conscience' sake. We know what is right when we love the law, having a conscious commitment to obey God. That is the higher and purer motive. And that's what Peter meant when he said, "Submit yourselves to every ordinance of man for the Lord's sake" (1 Pet. 2:13).

Do you obey the law because you're afraid of what will happen if you don't? Do you govern your life by fear, or do you think about obeying the law for the sake of honoring your Lord? The latter is the higher motive. We need both motivations, but I hope you're committed to the higher one. The conscience is that inner voice— that little place inside of us where God speaks of what is right and wrong. It is in the conscience that we should find our strongest motivation. There's no place for rebellion on the part of a Christian. We are to do what is right—submit.

Focusing on the Facts

1. To whom does the government become a terror (Rom. 13:3; see p. 39)?
2. Why do secular rulers know the difference between good and evil deeds (see pp. 39-40)?
3. What will the most evil society or the worst government hold to (see p. 40)?
4. In what ways will a government act towards evildoers when it fulfills its role to the maximum (see pp. 40-42)?
5. Why should government deal out equal retribution without pity (Deut. 19:20; see p. 41)?
6. What happens when a government doesn't fulfill its role as it should (see p. 42)?
7. How should you respond if government treats you badly? How did Paul and Silas respond (Acts 16:25; see pp. 42-43)?
8. What will those who do good receive from the government (Rom. 13:3; see p. 44)?
9. In what sense are all government officials servants of God (Rom. 13:4; see p. 44)?
10. If government acts as it should, why should people be afraid of it if they do evil (Rom. 13:4; see p. 45)?
11. When did God institute the death penalty (see p. 45)?
12. What are some of the crimes for which the Old Testament prescribed the death penalty (see p. 46)?

13. What act of God is government fulfilling when it uses capital punishment on evildoers (Rom. 12:19; see p. 47)?
14. What happens to a nation when it doesn't satisfy a death (see p. 47)?
15. Why did Abel's blood cry out to God (Gen. 4:10; see p. 47)?
16. What was God's primary reason for bringing judgment on the nation of Israel in the Babylonian captivity (Ezek. 7:23; see p. 48)?
17. Why does God want governments to utilize capital punishment (see pp. 49-50)?
18. What should be the Christian's highest motivation for submitting to the government (Rom. 13:5; see pp. 50-51)?

Pondering the Principles

1. Have you ever experienced unfair treatment from your government? Explain. How did you respond in that situation? What can you learn from the experience of Paul and Silas in Acts 16:25? Have you ever been protected by your government? Explain. Why is it to your benefit to submit to your government no matter how it treats you?

2. Does your government reward people for doing good? List some of the ways in which government rewards people. What is your response when you see the government praising someone for doing good? What should that make you want to do?

3. Based on this lesson, has your perspective of capital punishment changed or been strengthened? How has it changed? How has it been strengthened? If the issue of capital punishment came to a vote in your country or state, how would you vote?

4. Do you find yourself more committed to submit to the government out of fear or for the sake of your conscience? If to obey for the sake of conscience is the higher motive, then you need to take a closer look at the motive for your obedience. Ask God to help you to be more sensitive to His conviction. Each time you are called to submit to some institution of government, examine your motive for doing so. Seek to obey with the higher motive.

4

Paying Your Taxes—Part 1

Outline

Introduction

Lesson
I. The Principle (v. 6a)
   A. The Exploitation of Taxation
      1. Oppressive taxation
      2. Divisive taxation
      3. Intimidating taxation
   B. The Establishment of Taxation
      1. In Egypt
         a) The problem
         b) The plan
         c) The profit
         d) The performance
      2. In Israel
         a) The Lord's tithe
            (1) Supporting the priests
            (2) Sinning against God
         b) The festival tithe
         c) The welfare tithe
         d) The profit-sharing plans
            (1) Leviticus 19:9-10
            (2) Exodus 23:11
         e) The Temple tax
   C. The Explanation of Taxation
      1. The action of Christ
         a) The background of the question
            (1) The absurd request
            (2) The annual requirement
         b) The frankness of the answer
         c) The discussion of the issue

Introduction

Romans 13:6-7 is the setting for our message: "For, for this cause pay ye tribute also; for they are God's ministers, attending continually upon this very thing. Render, therefore, to all their dues: tribute to whom tribute is due; custom to whom custom; fear to whom fear; honor to whom honor."

It is a basic reality of human behavior that no one likes to pay taxes. Poor people don't like to pay taxes because they start out with so little money. When they have to pay taxes, they end up with even less. Rich people don't like to pay taxes because the more they have, the more tax they have to pay. Most everyone is negative about taxes. The United States was originally founded as a protest against taxation. It was born out of a revolution against taxation without representation.

We live in a society that doesn't like to pay taxes. It does everything it can to avoid paying them, both legally and illegally. What should the Christian's attitude be toward paying taxes, especially if we disagree with the government's usage of our tax money? What should we do if we disagree with its policies? If I send them my money, I'm allowing the government to use it in ways I might not agree with. We might also think that the present tax structure is unfair. Perhaps you think the escalating tax percentage based on income should be reduced to a common percent for everyone, no matter how much is earned. If we believe that the graduated tax program has the ultimate effect of penalizing the poor and stifling incentive in those who are more enterprising, shouldn't we have the right not to pay?

Even with all those criticisms, the Bible is explicit. Without equivocation it tells us to pay our taxes. It doesn't even qualify that statement. It doesn't say to pay them if you agree with what they're used for; it just says to pay your taxes. If we can come up with criticisms of our present tax structure, the people in the time of Paul could as well. Actually, their government was worse than ours in many ways. But that is never the issue. It wasn't the issue in the time of the Lord, and it isn't the issue today. The simple statement of Scripture is, "Pay your taxes."

We need to take a good look at what the Christian is to be responsible for in the matter of taxation. As we look at Romans 13:6-7, I want you to notice three things: the principle, the purpose, and then the particulars.

Lesson

I. THE PRINCIPLE (v. 6*a*)

"For, for this cause pay ye tribute also."

The Greek word for "tribute" is *phoros*, which basically refers to a tax levied against individual people. It isn't specific; it doesn't tell us what kind of tax, but it is referring to a personal tax. The word "also" reminds us that a Christian has two obligations to government. The first obligation is in verse 1, "Be subject unto the higher powers." Now Paul says, "Pay ye tribute also." These are the two basic responsibilities that a Christian has in human society: to submit to the government and pay taxes.

A. The Exploitation of Taxation

I want to develop this theme biblically. Taxation is not new to Romans 13. It is a very old biblical truth. Back in Genesis, we find systems of personal tax being levied against individuals within a given nation (Gen. 41, 47). In all periods of biblical history we can find taxation in government.

1. Oppressive taxation

Nehemiah 5:4 says, "There were also those who said, We have borrowed money for the king's tax, and that upon our lands and vineyards." The people were complaining that the taxes levied were so abusive that they had to mortgage their possessions to pay them. There were definitely times when the taxation system was oppressive.

2. Divisive taxation

Sometimes tax systems were very divisive. When they were abusive, they became divisive. For example, in 1 Kings 12 the kingdom of Israel had split into the Northern and Southern kingdoms. First Kings 12:4 says, "Thy father made our yoke grievous; now, therefore, make thou the grievous service of thy father, and his heavy yoke which he put on us, lighter, and we will serve thee." The people told Rehoboam that his father, Solomon, overtaxed them. They told him that if he didn't lower the taxes, they wouldn't serve him. He refused, and the kingdom split. So an unfair, unrealistic tax system can be divisive.

3. Intimidating taxation

We also find that some tax systems were designed to intimidate. Second Kings 23:35 says, "Jehoiakim . . . taxed the land to give the money according to the commandment of Pharaoh." That was pure intimidation. Pharaoh had a hold on Jehoiakim, who then taxed his people to pay for protection from Pharaoh—just as the Mafia extorts protection money from someone. Verse 35 continues, "He exacted the silver and the gold from the people of the land, of every one according to his valuation, to give it unto Pharaoh-neco."

The Bible records for us times when taxation was oppressive, divisive, and intimidating. Nonetheless, the command comes through unqualified. The Bible doesn't say if taxation is not oppressive, divisive, and intimidating, then pay it; it just says to pay your taxes. God recognizes that there will be times when taxation is inequitable, but the command still stands.

B. The Establishment of Taxation

1. In Egypt

The biblical teaching on taxation begins in Genesis 41:34 with the introduction of the first recorded national tax on personal income, property, and resources.

a) The problem

Pharaoh had a dream. In it were seven thin cows and seven fat cows. In his dream, the seven thin cows ate the seven fat cows. Then he dreamed about seven thin ears of grain that devoured seven fat ears of grain. Pharaoh was at a loss to interpret his dream (Gen. 41:1-8). But Joseph was able to interpret it for him. The seven skinny cows eating the seven fat cows and the seven thin ears of grain eating the seven fat ears of grain indicated that there would be seven years of plenty followed by seven years of famine (vv. 29-30).

a) The plan

How were they going to prepare for the seven years of famine? Joseph's plan is indicated in verse 34, "Let Pharaoh do this, and let him appoint officers over the land, and take up the fifth part of the land of Egypt in the seven plenteous years." Twenty percent of everyone's agricultural profit was laid in store for use during the seven years of famine. That was the initiation of the first recorded personal taxation system in a nation. And this was a pagan nation, not Israel. Egypt did not worship God. Nonetheless, taxation was an institution of God begun by God's choice servant Joseph to the advantage of Pharaoh and his land.

c) The profit

Verses 53-56 say, "And the seven years of plenteousness, that was in the land of Egypt, were ended. And the seven years of famine began to come, according as Joseph had said: and the famine was in all lands; but in all the land of Egypt there was bread. And when all the land of Egypt was famished, the people cried to Pharaoh for bread: and Pharaoh said unto all the Egyptians, Go unto Joseph; what he saith to you, do. And the famine was over all the face of the earth. And Joseph opened all the storehouses, and sold unto the Egyptians; and the famine was severe in the land of Egypt." When the famine became severe, the government provided what the people needed and made an immense profit. Verse 57 says, "All countries came into Egypt to Joseph to buy grain; because the famine was so severe in all lands."

d) The performance

Genesis 47:13-14 says, "There was no bread in all the land; for the famine was very severe, so that the land of Egypt and all the land of Canaan fainted by reason of the famine. And Joseph gathered up all the money that was found in the land of Egypt, and in the land of Canaan, for the grain which they bought; and Joseph brought the money into Pharaoh's house." Then verse 26 says, "Joseph made it a law over the land of Egypt unto this day, that Pharaoh should have the fifth part; except the land of the priests only, which became not Pharaoh's." Religious officials were set aside from taxation, but everyone else paid a tax of 20 percent. That became Egyptian law.

You say, "How do you know taxation was an institution of God?" Because God's servant Joseph instituted it. God was setting a pattern for future governments. The resources of their people could be collected and then distributed back to them when there was a need. Government is truly an institution of God, and it incorporated the concept of taxation as early as the book of Genesis.

2. In Israel

When God established the nation of Israel, did He have a taxation system?

a) The Lord's tithe

Leviticus 27 records the initiation of a taxation system in the nation of Israel. It became an essential part of life. Verses 30-31 say, "All the tithe [a tenth] of the land, whether of the seed of the land, or of the fruit of the tree, it is the Lord's: it is holy unto the Lord. And if a man will at all redeem any of his tithes, he shall add thereto the fifth part thereof." If you said, "I don't want to give any grain; I would like to give money instead," then you had to add a fifth to the tenth because they wanted the actual commodity. They were to give a tenth of everything each year. This tax was called the Lord's tithe because it was holy to the Lord (v. 30). It was even called the Levite tithe because the tenth was given to the Levites (Num. 18:21-24).

(1) Supporting the priests

Who were the Levites? Levi was one of the twelve tribes of Israel. When the land was divided among the tribes, the Levites received no land because they were not to be agriculturists. They were to be priests attending to matters of worship. As priests, they could not support themselves, so they were supported by the people. That same design of taxation was used in the pagan nation of Egypt. Their priests did not pay taxes either. In the nation of Israel the people paid taxes that went to the Levites. Why? Because as priests, they functioned as rulers, judges, and leaders of the nation.

The chief priests had been put in charge of maintaining the government as far back as the time of Moses. They were the judges, authorities, and rulers. Since they made decisions on behalf of the people, they were to be supported in that theocracy by the Lord's tithe, the 10 percent tax that was given every year.

(2) Sinning against God

If someone didn't give the Lord's tithe, he was committing a serious sin. In the third chapter of Malachi the prophet condemns the people in Israel because they didn't pay it. Verses 8-9 say, "Will a man rob God? Yet ye have robbed me. But ye say, How have we robbed thee? In tithes and offerings. Ye are cursed with a curse; for ye have robbed me, even this whole nation." They had the same problem we have today—they didn't pay their taxes. They didn't have a 93 billion dollar tax gap, but they had a very large one. In verse 10 God says, "Bring all the tithes into the storehouse [the treasury], that there may be food in mine house, and test me now herewith, saith the Lord of hosts, if I will not open for you the windows of heaven, and pour out for you a blessing, that there shall not be room enough to receive it." So God says, "Because you robbed Me, you cheated yourself out of blessing."

Remember, the Lord's tithe had nothing to do with free-will giving; it was a straight tax of 10 percent.

b) The festival tithe

Deuteronomy 12:10-11 says, "When ye go over the Jordan, and dwell in the land which the Lord your God giveth you to inherit, and when he giveth you rest from all your enemies round about, so that ye dwell in safety, then there shall be a place which the Lord your God shall choose to cause his name to dwell there [the Temple]; there shall ye bring all that I command you: your burnt offerings, and your sacrifices, your tithes, and the heave offering of your hand, and all your choice vows which ye vow unto the Lord." Then verses 17-18 say, "Thou mayest not eat within thy gates the tithe of thy grain, or of thy wine, or of thy oil, or the firstlings of thy herds or of

59

thy flock, nor any of thy vows which thou vowest, nor thy freewill offerings, or heave offering of thine hand; but thou must eat them before the Lord thy God in the place which the Lord thy God shall choose, thou, and thy son, and thy daughter, and thy manservant, and thy maidservant, and the Levite who is within thy gates; and thou shalt rejoice before the Lord thy God and all that thou puttest thine hands unto."

That was known as the festival tithe—another annual 10 percent tax on grain, wine, oil, firstlings of the herd or flock, and anything else that fell under its scope. What was this tenth for? The tithe was taken to a proper place in Jerusalem, where it was eaten by all the families of Israel and the Levites. It was a national potluck. These festivals were held periodically during the year. The intention was to support national worship, perpetuate the community of people, bring about national unity, and cultivate the social and cultural life of the Jewish nation—an essential element of national unity and richness of life.

The first tenth went to support the national government—to provide the food and resources needed by the people who ran the nation. The second tenth went to cultivate the cultural and national life. Our own taxes are used in much the same way. All the things we enjoy as a nation are provided through tax money.

c) The welfare tithe

Deuteronomy 14:28-29 says, "At the end of three years thou shalt bring forth all the tithe of thine increase the same year, and shalt lay it up within thy gates: and the Levite (because he has no part nor inheritance with thee), and the sojourner, and the fatherless [the orphan], and the widow, who are within thy gates, shall come, and shall eat and be satisfied; that the Lord thy God may bless thee in all the work of thine hand which thou doest." Every time God gave Israel a tax, He promised that if they paid it He would bless them. This third tax they paid at the end of every third year.

The Israelites paid a tenth for their government, a

tenth for their festivals, and another 3 1/3 percent for welfare, or approximately 23 percent a year in taxes. That is not unlike the original tax that was begun in Egypt, which was 20 percent. The three tithes were important. The first one paid for the needs of those who governed the nation. The second one cultivated national life. And the third one took care of the poor, the orphans, and the widows. It was a welfare tithe. Those three tithes were collected off the top of everyone's blessings and were used to strengthen the nation.

d) The profit-sharing plans

There were other provisions that the law of God indicated had to be made so that the resources could be matched with the needs.

(1) Leviticus 19:9-10—"When ye reap the harvest of your land, thou shalt not wholly reap the corners of thy field, neither shall thou gather the gleanings of thy harvest (v. 9). In other words, "When you go through your field, don't try to take every piece out of every corner. Whatever you might leave or miss, don't go back and collect it." Verse 10 says, "And thou shalt not glean thy vineyard, neither shalt thou gather every grape of thy vineyard; thou shalt leave them for the poor and sojourner: I am the Lord your God." That was a profit-sharing plan. When harvest time came, they took all they could in the normal harvesting process, but they were not to go back for anything that was left. It could then be enjoyed by those who had very little. That was a provision of the Mosaic law. So in a sense that was another percentage of gain left for someone else.

(2) Exodus 23:11—Every seventh year the Israelites had to let the land "rest and lie still; that the poor of thy people may eat: and what they leave the beasts of the field shall eat." Have you ever seen a field that's continually planted, but one year it isn't? What happens? Quite often something grows anyway. In Israel, if a field was vacant, a poor man might find something in that field to survive. What the poor didn't glean, the animals could have. Again, that was another way of

sharing the blessing of resources with those who were less privileged.

e) The Temple tax

There was one other provision. According to Exodus 30:13, the people were required to pay a half-shekel tax for the operation of the Temple. It was very expensive to operate. Everyone paid a half-shekel.

The tax in Israel amounted to a tenth for the government, another tenth for the festivals, a tenth every third year for welfare, plus what was left in the corners of the field, plus what grew when the field wasn't planted in the seventh year, plus the half-shekel Temple tax. So the people were probably looking at a tax of between 23 and 25 percent, depending on how good they were at harvesting their fields.

What Is Freewill Giving?

The tithes that are discussed in the Old Testament are not to be considered as freewill giving. They have absolutely no parallel to giving in the church. The Old Testament does speak about every man giving as he wills in his heart (Ex. 25:2). That refers to gifts offered to the Tabernacle or the Temple. But the tithes did not refer to the spontaneous and sacrificial giving of Proverbs 3:9-10: "Honor the Lord with thy substance, and with the first fruits of all thine increase; so shall thy barns be filled with plenty, and thy presses shall burst out with new wine." When you give the Lord the best of what you have and the top of what you take in, you'll be blessed. That's what freewill giving is—being generous to God. But people in the Old Testament were required to pay taxes. If they didn't, they were robbing God and were in line for judgment (Mal. 3:8-10). If they paid them, they would be blessed by God.

C. The Explanation of Taxation

In the New Testament, we find that the Lord upholds the same standard.

1. The action of Christ

As we look at Matthew 17, Jesus is in the process of instructing His disciples. In verse 24 they come to the town of Capernaum, where Peter lived. Our Lord was Himself a resident there for a time. Capernaum was on the northernmost point of the Sea of Galilee, at the foot of the hills that sloped down from Lebanon to the north. Verse 24 says, "When they were come to Capernaum, they that received tribute money came to Peter, and said, Doth not your master pay tribute?"

a) The background of the question

The background of this situation is essential. Jesus previously had told the disciples that He was going to die. Verses 22-23 say, "While they abode in Galilee, Jesus said unto them, The Son of Man shall be betrayed into the hands of men, and they shall kill him, and the third day he shall be raised again. And they were exceedingly sorry." How was He going to die? In Matthew 16:21 Jesus tells the disciples that the elders, chief priests, and scribes will kill Him. The disciples would have to face the fact that He would die violently at the hands of the Jewish authorities.

(1) The absurd request

After Jesus and His disciples arrived in Capernaum, these very same authorities asked for money. They were not asking Him to support the Roman government; this is the Temple tax. We know that later on the coin needed for the tax was wonderfully provided (v. 27). But in verse 24 the authorities ask, "Doth not your master pay tribute?"

Think about this: Here were men collecting money to put into the Temple treasury. Thirty pieces of silver from that treasury would be paid to Judas for betraying Christ. Talk about giving your money to something you wouldn't want to support! Jesus was being asked to put money into a treasury that would fund the betrayal that would lead to His death. Furthermore, Jesus had one time cleansed out the Temple with a scourge (John 2:14-16). He let everyone know what He thought about what was being done to God's house. And before His death He would do it one more time, predicting its devastation and destruction. He would call it a den of thieves rather than a house of prayer (Matt. 21:12-13). Jesus had already taught that the day was coming when men would neither worship God at Mount Gerizim, as the Samaritans did, or at Jerusalem, as the Jews did (John 4:21). That whole system was coming to an end.

In spite of that, representatives functioning in response to the mandates of those in authority at the Temple came saying, "We need your money to support our Temple." Christ had cleansed and cursed the Temple. It would ultimately be destroyed. And the religious leaders would pay for His betrayal out of the Temple treasury.

(2) The annual requirement

How was Jesus going to respond? His response was important because every Jewish male was required to pay an annual half-shekel tax. It was called the "Double Drachma Tax." It was equal to two Greek *drachma*, or about two-days' wages. The authorities had the power to demand the tax be paid. If a man didn't pay it, the officials had the authority to take compensation out of his personal goods. The coin that was required (the *didrachma*) was not in use in that day, so it was common for two men to go together to pay one *stater* (equal to two *didrachmas*). It was paid before the Passover to provide for the special needs of preparing the Temple for the Passover season. It fascinates me that even after Titus destroyed the Temple in A.D. 70, he saw the tax as such a good thing that he made the Jews pay it anyway. It went into the Temple of Jupiter Capitolinus, according to first-century Jewish historian Josephus.

b) The frankness of the answer

The Temple tax collectors approached Peter and asked him if Jesus paid the *didrachma*. Now you might think there would be some equivocation on the part of Peter—that he might give some speech about why Jesus doesn't put money into something He doesn't believe in. But that wasn't his answer. Verse 25 says, "He saith, Yes." It was an unqualified answer; Jesus paid His taxes.

c) The discussion of the issue

(1) The question

Verse 25 continues, "And when he was come into the house, Jesus spoke first to him, saying, What thinkest thou, Simon?" Jesus read his mind. Peter didn't say what had just happened. After having met the tax collector in the street, Peter came through the door, and the Lord says, "Of whom do the kings of the earth take custom or tribute? Of their own sons, or of strangers?" Jesus read Peter's thoughts. Peter was probably saying to himself, "The Lord pays His taxes, but why?" So Jesus asks him this question

(2) The answer

The answer is obvious. The kings at that particular time of history exacted taxes from everyone but their own families. What's the point of taking taxes from one's own family? It would be pointless to tax oneself to put it back into one's own bank account. Verse 26 says, "Peter saith unto him, Of strangers. Jesus saith unto him, Then are the sons free."

(3) The reason

The illustration is perfect because the Temple was supposed to be the house of God, and Jesus was the Son of God. As such, God would not require Jesus to pay the tax, neither would He require any of His children to pay the tax. That's why there is no set amount for giving in the church. God doesn't tax His own family—we give what's in our heart to give. Jesus is saying that as children of God, we are not obligated to pay a tax that supports our family.

d) The demonstration of the purpose

But Jesus adds, "Notwithstanding, lest we should offend them, go thou to the sea, and cast an hook, and take up the fish that first cometh up. And when thou hast opened its mouth, thou shalt find a piece of money; that take, and give unto them for me and thee" (v. 27). That doesn't seem to be fair. We wouldn't mind if we could pull our tax money out of the mouth of a fish. The Lord is demonstrating that He was not obligated to pay the tax and neither was Peter. But He paid it so He wouldn't offend the Jewish authorities. Think of it. The Lord actually gave His tax money to an apostate religion that ultimately would execute Him. He gave it in support of a place holding public services that were a mockery to God— a place He called a den of thieves. But taxation was designed by God. Jesus was not about to start a tax revolt by offending everyone. He didn't want the spiritual issues to become clouded. It would be a horrible thing if Christians started an uprising over taxation and got their focus on something other than the spiritual dimension. So Jesus told Peter to pay the tax so that they wouldn't offend anyone. Then it would always be clear what His purpose and mes- sage was.

Let's look at the facts. Jesus paid the tax to the Temple when it was right. He took a whip and cleansed it when He had to. Because we pay our taxes doesn't mean we don't have a right to speak in holy indignation against the abuse of taxes. But we pay it, and then we say what needs to be said in the right place at the right time when the issues are moral and spiritual.

2. The attitude of Christ

   a) The political trap

   The setting for Matthew 22:15 is the Wednesday of Passion Week. Jesus was being confronted by the Pharisees in the Temple. They were trying to trap Him with many different questions. Verse 16 says, "They sent out unto him their disciples with the Herodians."

   (1) Set

   The Pharisees and Herodians hated each other. The Pharisees were anti-Herod, who was a vassal king and not a true Jew. He had been given the right to rule by the Romans. The Herodians belonged to the party of the Herods. They wanted the Herods in power. So they were pro-Roman. Therefore, they had to be deferential to the Romans. Because they were so pro-Roman, they were the hated enemies of the Pharisees, who were anti-Roman. Even though the Phari- sees and Herodians were miles apart politically, they came together on one thing: getting rid of

Jesus. They became strange bedfellows over the elimination of Jesus.

The Pharisees wanted to bring the Herodians into their scheme for this reason: If they could get Jesus to affirm that He protested the paying of taxes to Rome, they knew the Herodians would report that to the Romans. However, if the Pharisees reported it, the Romans would think it was some kind of trick. But the Pharisees knew Rome would trust the Herodians. That's why the Pharisees enlisted the help of the Herodians.

(2) Sprung

In verse 16 the Pharisees approached Jesus with flattery: "Master, we know that thou art true, and teachest the way of God in truth, neither carest thou for any man [You don't play favorites]; for thou regardest not the person of men." In other words, "You don't care what rank men have or how much money they have. You're just truthful and honest." After flattering Him they said, "Tell us, therefore, what thinkest thou? Is it lawful to give tribute unto Caesar, or not?" (v. 17). Of course the Pharisees said, "Don't pay taxes to Rome. That is putting money into the Roman government. Caesar claims to be a god, and that's idolatry. Don't support an idolatrous, pagan, apostate government." (The Roman emperor even took the liberty to pronounce absolution over sins, acting as a high priest.) So the Pharisees wouldn't think of paying taxes to Rome, although they may have had to under constraint. However, they would never have said that publicly. But they did want Jesus to say something against taxation so the Herodians would report Him.

The Pharisees' question was in regard to a personal tax collected by the Roman procurator—the one denarius poll tax every male had to pay. The Jews hated that tax. Many revolts occurred because of it. I believe the destruction of Jerusalem in A.D. 70 came about in part as a result of a tax revolt in A.D. 66. The revolutionaries who led the revolt were known as Zealots. They led all kinds of terrorist activities against the Romans.

b) The parallel transactions

(1) The principle affirmed

The Pharisees wanted Jesus to say, "Don't pay your taxes." Then the Herodians would report Him to the Romans, who would then treat Him like an insurrectionist. But they didn't get the answer they wanted: "Jesus perceived their wickedness, and said, Why test me, ye hypocrites? Show me the tribute money. And they brought unto him a denarius. And he saith unto them, Whose is this image and superscription?" (vv. 18-20). The picture was of the emperor, and he was designated on the coin as the high priest. Augustus even called himself the son of God. He wanted to be worshiped as deity—a serious issue of idolatry to the Jewish people. Verse 21 says, "They say unto him, Caesar's. Then saith he unto them, Render, therefore, unto Caesar the things which are Caesar's; and unto God, the things that are God's." Jesus was saying, "Pay your taxes to Caesar and give your worship to God." That is the principle affirmed throughout Scripture.

(2) The principle amplified

You may say, "But Caesar was an apostate. He called himself the son of God." That's true, and Jesus was telling them to give their taxes to a man who was claiming to be the son of God. Now, when anyone says, "I'm not going to pay my taxes because they fund abortions," they don't have a leg to stand on. We know abortion is wrong, and we need to speak against abortion and any other moral evil every time we have an opportunity. But that doesn't preclude the fact that we are obligated to pay our taxes, even as Jesus paid taxes to an apostate Roman government and encouraged the people to do the same. Any government, no matter how bad it is, is better than no government at all. And it is instituted by God for the protection and preservation of life and property. Jesus even paid a

Temple tax that could have been used for His own destruction.

The principle is very simple: Pay your taxes. I believe we can claim the same promises the Old Testament gave: When you pay your taxes, you can be sure God will bless you. I pay my taxes as an act of obedience to God, believing that in doing so God will bless me. I don't pay one penny more than the IRS tells me I have to pay, but I don't pay one penny less.

Focusing on the Facts

1. What does the Bible say we are to do, even though we may have criticisms about our tax structure (Rom. 13:6; see p. 54)?
2. What kind of tax is Romans 13:6 referring to (see p. 55)?
3. Describe some of the characteristics of various tax systems described by the Old Testament (see pp. 55-56).
4. What was Joseph's interpretation of Pharaoh's dream in Genesis 41:29-30 (see p. 56)?
5. How did Joseph solve the problem of preparing for the coming famine (Gen. 41:34; see p. 57)?
6. Describe how Joseph's taxation system became law in Egypt. How do we know that it was an institution of God (Gen. 47:26; see pp. 57-58)?
7. Describe the Lord's tithe (Lev. 27:30-31; see p. 58).
8. Why did the Levites need to receive the governmental tax (see pp. 58-59)?
9. What did God promise to do to those who paid the Lord's tithe (Mal. 3:8-10; see p. 59)?
10. Describe the festival tithe. What was its purpose (Deut. 12:17-18; see pp. 59-60)?
11. Explain the welfare tithe (Deut. 14:28-29; see p. 60).
12. Describe the different types of profit-sharing plans the nation of Israel supported (Lev. 19:9; Ex. 23:11; see p. 61).
13. What was the Temple tax (Ex. 30:13; see p. 62)?
14. What is freewill giving? Why doesn't it have anything to do with the tithes (Prov. 3:9-10; see p. 62)?
15. According to Matthew 16:21, how was Jesus going to be killed? Who was going to kill Him (see p. 63)?
16. Why might Jesus have had a problem with giving tax money to the Temple (see p. 63)?
17. Who was required to pay the Temple tax? What was the purpose of the tax (see p. 64)?
18. Did Jesus have to pay the Temple tax? Did Peter? Why did Jesus pay the tax (Matt. 17:25-27; see pp. 64-65)?

19. Explain the particulars of the trap that the Pharisees were setting against Jesus (Matt. 22:16-17; see p. 67).
20. What was Jesus' answer to the Pharisees? What principle was He affirming (Matt. 22:18-21; see p. 68)?

Pondering the Principles

1. What are some of the criticisms you have of your current tax system? Be specific. Do you think God would criticize the tax system the same way you do? In the light of Romans 13:6, what must your response be to your tax system? Imagine the worst possible tax system. If that system was adopted by your government, would your responsibility to pay your taxes change?

2. Many people have a tendency to confuse Old Testament tithes with freewill giving. Look up the following verses: Ex. 25:1-2; 35:4-10, 21-22; 36:5-7; Deut. 16:17; 1 Chron. 29:9, 16; Prov. 3:9-10; 11:24-25. Based on those verses, how would you define freewill giving? What happened to the people when they followed that pattern? Do you give with the attitude expressed in those verses? To help you in your desire to give to God, memorize these words of our Lord in Luke 6:38: "Give, and it will be given to you; good measure, pressed down, shaken together, running over, they will pour into your lap. For by your standard of measure it will be measured to you in return" (NASB*).

3. Read Matthew 22:20. Do you have the right balance in what you give to your government and what you give to God? How much time do you spend in efforts to effect political change, such as examining issues, writing letters to public officials, or taking part in political rallies? How much time do you spend worshiping God? If you find that those two things are out of balance, begin to devote more of your time to the Lord. Allow Him to govern your time and to give you the proper perspective of your government.

*New American Standard Bible.

5
Paying Your Taxes—Part 2

Outline

Introduction
A. The Problems
   1. Sin
   2. Satan
     a) He intensifies sin
     b) He controls the world
       (1) Matthew 4:9
       (2) 1 John 5:19
       (3) Luke 4:6
       (4) John 12:31
B. The Paradox

Review
I. The Principle (v. 6*a*)

Lesson
II. The Purpose (v. 6*b*)
A. Serving a Divine Purpose
   1. The minimizing of God's standard
   2. The models of order and peace
     a) Justin Martyr
     b) Tertullian
B. Ruling Under a Divine Trust
C. Attending to Divine Service
   1. The choice of servants
   2. The commitment of servants
     a) Recognition
     b) Responsibility
       (1) Serve a divine purpose
       (2) Be committed to truth and justice
       (3) Maintain order
       (4) Avoid self-seeking

(5) Sympathize with the needy
(6) Treat others with kindness
(7) Speak the truth
(8) Enforce public morality
III. The Particulars (v. 7)
  A. The General Obligation (v. 7*a*)
  B. The Specific Obligations (v. 7*b*)
    1. "Tribute to whom tribute"
    2. "Custom to whom custom"
    3. "Fear to whom fear"
    4. "Honor to whom honor"

Introduction

A. The Problems

Our world is in a terrible condition. Reading the local newspaper can be a distressing and discouraging experience. We're all aware of the conflicts, revolutions, and wars occurring throughout the world. An unending conflict rages on every level, but particularly in the hearts of individuals. Many people can't cope with life to a degree never before experienced in human history. It seems as though mental illness is at an all-time high. It begins with an individual who can't get along with himself, which progresses then to his spouse, family, neighbors, country, and finally his world. We hear many solutions offered to correct these problems. Most think the reasons for our problems are political or economic, such as a bad economy, unwise leadership, social injustice, and various ideologies and philosophies. It is claimed that if all these things could somehow be altered, we could clean up our perspectives on life and begin to deal with our problems.

The truth is that all our problems stem from two things: sin and Satan. The Bible is very clear about that.

1. Sin

  Man is hopelessly engulfed in a state of sinfulness. It is because of his sinfulness that he does what he does. He is bound to a depravity that has reached the very base of his existence. Sin is man's basic problem.

2. Satan

  I would add that Satan is also a problem because he provokes sin. He has a way of exciting the senses through his control of the world, and that causes men to step into sin. Ephesians 2:2 says that men are victims of "the prince of the power of the air, the spirit that now worketh in the sons of disobedience."

a) He intensifies sin

Since man is a sinner, he finds himself in the domain of Satan, where his tendency toward sin is excited by Satan's influence. Satan is an incorrigible rebel—an inveterate criminal. Because Satan dominates the world of man, the problem is not simply human; it is supernaturally intensified. Man is a product of his fallenness and satanic activity.

b) He controls the world

A look through the pages of Scripture will make us aware that Satan is in control of our world.

(1) Matthew 4:9—Satan had just shown Jesus all the kingdoms of the world. Then he said, "All these things will I give thee, if thou wilt fall down and worship me." That indicates to me that Satan possessed the various kingdoms of the world.

(2) 1 John 5:19—"The whole world lieth in wickedness."

(3) Luke 4:6—In his account of the temptation of Christ, Luke says, "The devil said unto him, All this authority will I give thee, and the glory of them [the kingdoms of the world]; for that is delivered unto me, and to whomsoever I will I give it." Satan is in charge of the kingdoms of the world and has the prerogative to give them to whomever he wants. That's an important perception.

(4) John 12:31—Jesus said, "Now is the judgment of this world; now shall the prince of this world be cast out." With His own mouth, Jesus affirmed the monarchy that Satan has over this world. In a certain sense, it is Satan's world. Jesus also called him the prince of this world in John 14:30 and John 16:11.

Satan is in charge of the kingdoms of the world. He has the right to give those kingdoms to whomever he chooses.

B. The Paradox

Although national governments are ordained by God (Rom. 13:1), nonetheless they express Satan's influence and activity. This demonic activity is kept in check by those governments, yet in some sense governments are under the control of Satan. It is an interesting paradox. God has ordained government for the preservation of man. But man is basically evil, and his government is also evil. Satan is active and aggressive in human government, yet he is limited by God because He has established government to preserve human society. So while we say that the governments of the nations of the world are ordained by God, we are not saying they are necessarily being run by God or are reflective of His will. Since man has unlimited potential for evil, which is incited by the world and the flesh, government is an essential restraint. God has ordained it to restrain the satanic activity inherent within each nation.

Review

God ordains government. What does He call us to do in response to it? First, Romans 13:1 calls us to be subject to the government. Second, Romans 13:6-7 calls us to support the government. We submit to government because it is ordained of God. That doesn't mean it isn't satanic. That doesn't mean it reflects always the will of God. It simply means that God has ordained government to hold in check the limitless evil of Satan, his demons, and men. We are called to submit to those who are in authority: "For there is no power but of God; the powers that be are ordained of God" (Rom. 13:1). We have learned in Romans 13:1-5 that we are to submit to the government. Now we are learning in verses 6-7 that we are to support the government.

I. THE PRINCIPLE (v. 6*a*; see pp. 55-69)

"For, for this cause pay ye tribute also."

Lesson

II. THE PURPOSE (v. 6*b*)

"For they are God's ministers, attending continually upon this very thing."

We are to pay our taxes because those who collect them are God's ministers. That takes us back to verse 4, "For he is the minister of God to thee for good . . . the minister of God, an avenger to execute wrath upon him that doeth evil." Those who are in authority are either ministers of God for good or wrath, depending on how you respond to them.

A. Serving a Divine Purpose

The Greek word in verse 6 for "ministers" is *leitourgos*, from which we get the word *liturgy*. It speaks of religious service to God. It is used in Hebrews 1:7 of the service of angels: "And of the angels he saith, Who maketh his angels spirits, and his ministers [Gk., *leitourgos*] a flame of fire." Angels are called ministers in the sense of their religious service to God. Verse 14 says angels are "ministering spirits, sent forth to minister." Again, the same word for minister is used. There are different words for ministry, but Paul chose the word that referred to a ministry specifically to God.

We learn then that public servants who exercise authority in a national government are, in a unique sense, serving God. They perform an act of religious service because government is ordained by God, and resistance to it is resistance to God. We are to support the government by paying our taxes because it is serving God. Government is ordained by God for the preservation of life and property. Those who serve in it, who collect our taxes to keep the government functioning, do so as ministers of God. That doesn't mean they're all Christians and that they do all they ought to do. But it does mean that government serves a divine purpose.

1. The minimizing of God's standard

Robert Culver is correct when he says, "Where theistic religion grows weak, [justice] will weaken. Crimes then are defined as antisocial activity, which in turn is then merely what the majority says it is. Then punishments seem to be the result of the majority's ganging up on the minority. This in turn seems inconsistent with democratic feelings. The result is a decline in uniform application of penalties for crime, resultant miscarriage of justice, trampling on the rights of law-abiding people, together with an increase in what ought to be called crime" (*Toward a Biblical View of Civil Government* [Chicago: Moody, 1974], pp. 78-79). He's right. As soon as the principles of government are detached from God and no longer seen as a reflection of the divine mind, justice weakens. We are seeing that in our society. Crimes no longer are defined as crimes but as anti-social behavior. The question isn't, Are you guilty? but, Were you psychologically sound when you did it?

The Bible knows nothing of that. If you committed a crime, you paid a penalty whether you were psychologically sound or not. This is an issue now because society sees crime as anti-social behavior rather than a reaction against a holy law. We no longer see God's holy standard behind our laws. As a result, punishment does seem to be the result, as Culver says, "of the majority's ganging up on the minority." Now everyone wants to fight for the rights of the criminal, and there are miscarriages of justice and an increase in crime.

Every principle of justice and social order must be based on the rock bed of righteousness. When the foundation of what is right and wrong is removed, all that's left is the opinion of the majority. The result is a loss of justice. Government should not only be a service to God but also be based on the standards that God has established. Since there is a divine purpose behind government, we ought to do all we can to maintain a godly standard. That's why we should take issue with the morality of our time. When it begins to decline, we lose our foundation. But even when government abandons a biblical foundation, our orders are the same—we are to submit to it and support it with our taxes.

2. The models of order and peace

    The apostle Paul wanted Christianity to avoid insurrectionist, Judaistic attitudes of rebellion against the government. Christians are bound together by a common commitment to be models of order and peace. That's exactly what Christians were in the early days of the church. In spite of hostile and persecuting governments, they maintained a marvelous testimony of integrity by submitting to the government and paying their taxes.

    a) Justin Martyr

        There was a man who lived from around A.D. 100 to 163 by the name of Justin Martyr. He is well-known among theologians. In his First Apology he said, "Everywhere, we, more readily than all men, endeavour to pay to those appointed by you the taxes both ordinary and extraordinary, as we have been

76

taught by [Jesus]. . . . Whence to God alone we render worship, but in other things we gladly serve you, acknowledging you as kings, and rulers of men, and praying that with your kingly power you be found to possess also sound judgment" (chap. xvii). That should be the Christian's attitude. We give our worship to God, but we'll support our government also.

b) Tertullian

Tertullian was a Carthaginian theologian who lived from around A.D. 160 to 230. He wrote in his *Apology*, "Without ceasing, for all our emperors we offer prayer. We pray for life prolonged; for security to the empire; for protection to the imperial house; for brave armies, a faithful senate, a virtuous people, the world at rest—whatever, as man or Caesar, an emperor would wish" (chap. xxx). He knew the emperor was called by the Lord to his office. Tertullian had the right attitude, even in a time when the empire was hostile toward Christians.

That was the spirit Paul was after. And that spirit did reside in the leaders of the church in those early centuries; it should reside in us as well. Jesus taught that we are to respect the government, and Paul adds we are to do so because they are the ministers of God.

B. Ruling Under a Divine Trust

We have to keep in mind that all authority in government is delegated from the Lord. It is important for us to remind our leaders that they have a divine trust granted to them by God. In that sense, they rule under Him.

There is a most interesting section in the Psalms, running from chapters 92 to 98. There is a recurring theme through these psalms, testifying to the world that God is the only true sovereign and King, and that all other authority is simply delegated from Him.

1. Psalm 92:8—"But thou, Lord, art most high for evermore."

2. Psalm 93:1-2—"The Lord reigneth; he is clothed with majesty. The Lord is clothed with strength, wherewith he hath girded himself; the world also is established, that it cannot be moved. Thy throne is established of old; thou art from everlasting."

3. Psalm 94:1-2, 10—"O Lord God, to whom vengeance belongeth; O God, to whom vengeance belongeth, show thyself. Lift up thyself, thou judge of the earth. . . . He who chastiseth the nations, shall not he correct? He who teacheth man knowledge, shall not he know?" God is always exalted as the sovereign.

4. Psalm 95:3-7—"The Lord is a great God, and a great King above all gods. In his hand are the deep places of the earth; the strength of the hills is his also. The sea is his, and he made it, and his hands formed the dry land. Oh, come, let us worship and bow down; let us kneel before the Lord our maker. For he is our God, and we are the people of his pasture, and the sheep of his hand."

5. Psalm 96:3-10—"Declare his glory among the nations, his wonders among all peoples. For the Lord is great, and greatly to be praised; he is to be feared above all gods. For all the gods of the nations are idols; but the Lord made the heavens. Honor and majesty are before him; strength and beauty are in his sanctuary. Give unto the Lord, O ye kindreds of the peoples; give unto the Lord glory and strength. Give unto the Lord the glory due unto his name; bring an offering, and come into his courts. Oh, worship the Lord in the beauty of holiness; fear before him, all the earth. Say among the nations that the Lord reigneth."

6. Psalm 97:1, 5-6—"The Lord reigneth; let the earth rejoice. . . . The hills melted like wax at the presence of the Lord, at the presence of the Lord of the whole earth. The heavens declare his righteousness, and all the peoples see his glory."

7. Psalm 98:2, 9—"The Lord hath made known his salvation; his righteousness hath he openly shown in the sight of the nations. . . . He cometh to judge the earth."

8. Psalm 83:1-7, 13, 17-18—"Keep not thou silence, O God; hold not thy peace, and be not still, O God. For, lo, thine enemies make a tumult, and they that hate thee have lifted up the head. They have taken crafty counsel against thy people, and consulted against thy hidden ones. They have said, Come, and let us cut them off from being a nation; that the name of Israel may be no more in remembrance. For they have consulted together with one consent; they are confederate against thee: the tabernacles of Edom, and the Ishmaelites; of Moab, and the

Hagarenes; Gebal, and Ammon, and Amalek; the Philistines with the inhabitants of Tyre. . . . O my God, make them like a wheel, like the stubble before the wind. . . . Let them be confounded and troubled forever; yea, let them be put to shame, and perish, that men may know that thou, whose name alone is the Lord, art the Most High over all the earth."

9. Daniel 4:32—King Nebuchadnezzar was told, "They shall drive thee from men, and thy dwelling shall be with the beasts of the field; they shall make thee to eat grass like oxen, and seven times shall pass over thee, until thou know that the Most High ruleth in the kingdom of men, and giveth it to whomsoever he will." Nebuchadnezzar thought he was invincible. He thought he had obtained his kingdom by his own power and wisdom. But he was going to learn a lesson by becoming a raving maniac and living like an animal, his hair growing like a bird's feathers and his fingernails like eagles' claws. He learned that God gives and takes kingdoms according to His will.

10. Daniel 5:21—This verse describes again what King Nebuchadnezzar was taught: "Till he knew that the Most High God ruled in the kingdom of men, and that he appointeth over it whomsoever he will." If a person is in a position of authority, that's because God delegated that right to him. It is a divine privilege and a divine occupation.

C. Attending to Divine Service

In Romans 13:6 Paul says rulers "are God's ministers, attending continually upon this very thing." What thing? The service of ruling; the service of leading people, protecting them, collecting their taxes, and performing all civil matters for the public good.

1. The choice of servants

When we have the opportunity to vote for officials, we need to choose those who are competent and committed to serve. If you find someone in office who is unfaithful and isn't continually attending to service but is attending to something else, we need to find another servant. It would be best if they were Christians, but we often don't have that alternative, so we choose someone who's competent.

If I was going to have heart surgery, it would be wonderful to have a heart surgeon who is a Christian. But if I had my choice between an incapable Christian surgeon and a skilled, unsaved heart surgeon, I'd take the skilled, unsaved surgeon. There may come a time in government when our choice is between a competent person and an incompetent one. There may be times when a Christian is the incompetent and unfaithful one. We have to be careful to know whom we are selecting. We want people who understand something of the dilemma Moses faced in Exodus 18. He couldn't get all the work done. He looked at everything he had to do in judging Israel, but he couldn't handle it. That's when his father-in-law told him to divide up the responsibility (vv. 14-23). Moses followed his father-in-law's advice and selected qualified people to handle all the varying responsibilities. He divided up his load and was therefore able to do it well (vv. 24-26). Government is called to do what it does well—to attend itself continually to ruling and protecting its people.

2. The commitment of servants

To satisfy my own heart and mind, I spent some time looking through the prophets because they have so much to say to leaders. We've said that we need to be willing to submit and pay our taxes—that's our part. But we should also note what the leaders' part is.

a) Recognition

First, they are to recognize that they are in leadership because God put them there. They need to know that their responsibility was delegated to them by divine authority. They certainly should take stock of the divine standard. They ought to be faithful knowing that their accountability is to God.

b) Responsibility

Scripture is explicit about the kind of people who are to be in government leadership. No matter if you read Isaiah, Jeremiah, Ezekiel, Daniel, Hosea, Joel, Amos, Obadiah, Jonah, Micah, Nahum, Habakkuk, Zephaniah, Haggai, Zechariah, or Malachi, they all spoke not only to Israel but also to all the nations around Israel. They were calling for leaders of all nations to conform to a divine standard.

I want to give you some principles that we need to lay

upon our leaders if they're going to be faithful in their responsibility. Jeremiah 1:9-10 says, "Then the Lord put forth his hand, and touched my mouth. And the Lord said unto me, Behold, I have put my words in thy mouth. See, I have this day set thee over the nations and over the kingdoms, to root out, and to pull down, and to destroy, and to throw down, to build, and to plant." Jeremiah's message went far beyond Israel. God has requirements of all national leaders, not just those in Israel. And it was not only Jeremiah who gave that message, but many other prophets did as well. What does God require of the rulers of nations?

(1) Serve a divine purpose

First, God requires leaders to know that they serve a divine purpose. God told Nebuchadnezzar that he would have to learn the hard way that God was the Most High ruler who gives kingdoms to whom He wills. Any ruler from the president down to a local assemblyman needs to know that his responsibility is God-given.

(2) Be committed to truth and justice

The prophets made it very clear that one called to leadership is to be humble, serious, diligent, and loyal to truth and justice. If leaders know they serve a divine purpose, they ought to serve in a manner that reflects that knowledge. Daniel rebuked Nebuchadnezzar for his pride (Dan. 4:25-26) and for oppressing the poor (Dan. 4:27). Daniel pronounced judgment on Belshazzar for his pride and his failure to glorify God (Dan. 5). God indicts the leaders beyond Israel.

I believe that while we are to submit to our rulers, they are called to accountability before God. While we are to be willing to submit to the authorities, we also have to be willing to confront their evil if it needs to be confronted. If we are going to be faithful and be the right kind of citizens, we will submit. But when the leaders perpetrate evil, vice, wickedness, and self-seeking policies, we need to speak out with a prophetic voice.

81

(3) Maintain order

The prophets taught that leaders should maintain order by a just and firm enforcement of the law. The prophets indicted the nations for failing to enforce the law—allowing people to get away with crimes without punishment. That is particularly true in Jeremiah's prophecy. Jeremiah 34:8-9 says, "This is the word that came unto Jeremiah from the Lord, after King Zedekiah had made a covenant with all the people who were at Jerusalem, to proclaim liberty unto them, that every man should let his manservant, and every man his maidservant, being an Hebrew or an Hebrewess, go free; that none should enslave them, to wit, a Jew his brother." A decree was made to free those people. But verse 11 says, "Afterward they turned, and caused the servants and the handmaids, whom they had let go free, to return, and brought them into subjection for servants and for handmaids." The people were supposed to let their servants go free, but they didn't. They took them back. The rest of the story chronicles that there was no enforcement of the decree. Because of that, God said, "Ye turned and polluted my name. . . . I will command, saith the Lord, and cause them [Judah's enemies] to return to this city; and they shall fight against it, and take it, and burn it with fire; and I will make the cities of Judah a desolation without an inhabitant" (vv. 16, 22). One of the reasons for the terrible captivity that came upon Israel was that they were not enforcing the covenants they had made. Leaders are responsible to enforce the law firmly and justly.

(4) Avoid self-seeking

Leader are not to be preoccupied with their own welfare and position. Jeremiah 22:13-15 says, "Woe unto him who buildeth his house by unrighteousness, and his chambers by wrong; who useth his neighbor's service without wages, and giveth him not for his work; who saith, I will build myself a wide house and large chambers, and cutteth out windows; and it is paneled with cedar, and painted with vermilion. Shalt thou reign, because thou closest thyself in cedar? Did not thy father eat and drink, and do justice and righteousness, and then it was well with him?" This message is being given to wicked King Jehoiakim. Then verse 17 says, "But thine eyes and thine heart are not but for thy covetousness, and for shedding innocent blood, and for oppression, and for violence, to do it." When a leader is covetous, self-seeking, violent, and oppressive, the judgment of God will fall. They are not to seek their own welfare at the expense of others. There are leaders around the world that do that, and they are under the condemnation of Scripture.

(5) Sympathize with the needy

Those who serve in an official capacity should care for people who have needs. Isaiah 10:1-2 says, "Woe unto them who decree unrighteous decrees, and who write grievousness which they have prescribed, to turn aside the needy from justice, and to take away the right from the poor of my people, that widows may be their prey, and that they may rob the fatherless!" Israel had leaders who were unbelievably brutal, depriving the poor and needy (cf. Amos 2:6-7).

(6) Treat others with kindness

A leader should have an attitude of basic decency toward people. That principle is violated by the tyrants, despots, and murderous leaders of the world. Amos 1:13 says, "They have ripped up the women with child in Gilead." The people of Ammon ripped open the wombs of pregnant women.

(7) Speak the truth

Leaders must speak truth. God hates lying lips. Amos 2:4-5 says, "For three transgressions of Judah, and for four, I will not turn away its punishment, because they have despised the law of the Lord, and have not kept his commandments, and their lies caused them to err, after which their fathers have walked; but I will send a fire upon Judah, and it shall devour the palaces of Jerusalem." God indicted the leaders for their lying tongues.

(8) Enforce public morality

To be faithful to their delegated authority from God, leaders must enforce public morality. We see them failing to do that today. God sent Jonah to Nineveh and said, "Cry against it; for their wickedness is come up before me" (Jonah 1:2). God indicted that city and all its leaders for tolerating wickedness. He promised devastating judgment if Nineveh did not repent. Isaiah 13-23 is a cry against the leaders for failing to call the people to a high moral standard.

Scripture indicates some very specific things that leaders are to do. Let me briefly review them: Leaders need to know that they serve a divine purpose. They are to be humble, serious, diligent, and loyal to truth and justice. If they know their service is rendered to God, then they ought to take it very seriously. They are to maintain order by a just and firm enforcement of the law. They are not to seek their own welfare. They should sympathize with the needy. They are to treat others with kindness. They must always speak the truth. Finally, they are to enforce public morality.

The Bampton Lectures of 1898

Robert Lawrence Ottley in his Bampton Lectures of 1898 had some interesting things to say that relate to what we have been studying. (The Bampton Lectures were a series of eight lectures on theological topics given regularly at Oxford University.) Ottley said, "The Old Testament may be studied . . . as an instructor in social Righteousness. It exhibits the moral government of God as attested in his dealings with nations rather than with individuals; and it was their consciousness of the action and presence of God in history that made the prophets preachers . . . to the world at large. . . . There is indeed significance in the fact that in spite of their ardent zeal for social reform they did not as a rule take part in political life or demand political reforms. They desired . . . not better institutions, but better men" (*Aspects of the Old Testament*, The Bampton Lectures, 1897 [London: Longmans, 1898], pp. 430-31). I believe that in our day the church and its preachers have to rise to the level of not seeking political reform but calling for better men. They should not try to manipulate the system but confront its evil. Although we want to be submissive, we will not be silent when the role of leadership is abused.

We support government by paying our taxes because we realize that its leaders are God's ministers called to attend continually to their service. If they don't attend continually to it, we are responsible to bring it to their attention.

III. THE PARTICULARS (v. 7)

Paul now gets more specific in his command so we can be sure we understand the fullness of our obligation.

A. The General Obligation (v. 7a)

"Render, therefore, to all their dues."

The word "render" is *apodidomi* in the Greek text. It refers to giving back something that you owe. That's what you do when you pay your taxes. You owe taxes; you're not giving them as a gift. When you render something, you are paying back a debt (cf. Matt. 5:26; 18:25-26, 28-30, 34; 20:8; 22:21). The word "dues" is *opheilē* in the Greek text. It means "a debt" or "an obligation." Pay your debt to the government. We have a moral obligation to do so. Romans 13:8 says, "Owe no man any thing"—and that includes the government. Verse 7 says, "Render, therefore, to all their dues." Taxes are debts owed. If you don't pay, you're a robber.

B. The Specific Obligations (v. 7b)

1. "Tribute to whom tribute."

"Tribute" is *phoros* in the Greek text. Rome had one tax called *kensos* in Greek, and that was a head tax, or census. Every person paid it. Then they had the poll tax, or land tax. That is what Paul is referring to in verse 7. This tax was like our income tax. An assessment was made on land, property, slaves, and capital. The taxable amount of one's possessions was determined, the appropriate tax rate applied, and then the person was charged the tax. So Paul says to pay your income tax.

2. "Custom to whom custom."

The word "custom" is *telos* in the Greek text. It refers to revenue that was raised from merchandise or goods. It would be like duty or sales tax—any tax attached to a commodity. Paul is saying to pay your sales tax or your duty. Don't smuggle things; pay what's fair. Tax collectors were positioned at all crossroads. That's what Matthew did, sit at crossroads collecting taxes and duties from people transferring goods across borders.

3. "Fear to whom fear."

The Greek word for fear is *phobos*, from which we get the English word *phobia*. It can mean anything from respect to sheer terror, depending on how it's used. It is translated "terror" in Romans 13:3: "For rulers are not a terror to good works, but to the evil." It means "respect" in verse 7. You ought to have a healthy respect for the people who collect your taxes. That healthy respect translates into giving them what you owe them, realizing they have a right to it for the service they render. First Peter 2:17-18 says, "Honor all men. Love the brotherhood. Fear God. Honor the king. Servants, be subject to your masters." Show people respect for the position of authority they possess.

4. "Honor to whom honor."

The Greek word for honor is *timē*. It can sometimes refer to money. So this phrase could be translated, "Give money to whom money is due." It can also mean "respect." It is best to see Paul as using two words that refer to money—tax and duty—and two words that demonstrate attitude—respect and honor. We are to pay our taxes and duty with an attitude of respect and honor.

Notice this illustration: First Timothy 5:17 says, "Let the elders that rule well be counted worthy of double honor [*timē*]." What is the double honor? Verse 18 says, "For the scripture saith, Thou shalt not muzzle the ox that treadeth out the grain." In other words, if you expect an ox to tread the grain, you'd better feed him. So first of all, if you have an elder that rules well, pay him money. Then verse 19 says, "Against an elder receive not an accusation." That means he should be shown respect. But Paul goes on to say that if the elder does sin, he is to be rebuked before everyone (v. 20). Double honor would be respect and money.

As Christians, we are called to pay our taxes, respect our leaders, and give them the honor that is due them. We should want to do what is right by giving honor to whom honor is due and respect to whom respect is due. We should pay our taxes and live as Christians should live for the glory of our Lord.

Focusing on the Facts

1. What are the two sources of man's problems in the world (see pp. 72-73)?
2. How is Satan related to sin (see p. 73)?
3. Cite some Scriptures indicating that Satan is in control of the world (see p. 73).
4. Explain the paradox surrounding who controls government (see p. 74).
5. When Paul used the word "ministers" in Romans 13:6, what was he referring to (see p. 75)?
6. What happens when the principles of government are detached from God (see pp. 75-76)?
7. Explain how Christians in the early days of the church were models of order and peace (see pp. 76-77).
8. Cite some Scriptures testifying that God is the only true Sovereign and King (see pp. 77-79).
9. What kind of officials should Christians vote for (see p. 79)?
10. What is one important thing that the leaders in government need to recognize (see p. 80)?
11. What was one of the main messages that God wanted the prophets to communicate to the world (see pp. 80-81)?
12. What should Christians be willing to do when leaders perpetrate evil (see p. 81)?
13. What was one of the reasons that the nation of Israel was taken into captivity (see Jer. 34:8-9, 11, 16, 22; p. 82)?
14. Of what did Jeremiah accuse Jehoiakim (Jer. 22:13-15; see pp. 82-83)?
15. What was Judah indicted for in Amos 2:4-5 (see pp. 83-84)?
16. Why did God indict Nineveh and its leaders (Jonah 1:2; see p. 84)?
17. What did Paul mean when he said, "Render, therefore, to all their dues" (Rom. 13:7; see p. 85)?
18. Explain each of the specific obligations that Christians have to their government (Rom. 13:7; see pp. 85-86).

Pondering the Principles

1. How are you presently fulfilling your responsibility to be a model of order and peace? Both Justin Martyr and Tertullian testified to the ways in which they tried to be models (see pp. 76-77). Compare what you are doing to what they practiced: They paid

taxes that were ordinary and extraordinary, worshiped God only, and served the government. They also prayed for kings and rulers in these ways: for prolonged life, sound judgment, security for the nation, protection for the leaders, a faithful senate, a virtuous people, and a world at peace. If you have not been a model in those ways, make the commitment that the members of the early church did.

2. When you choose leaders in an election, what criteria do you use? Review the section on the responsibility of leaders (pp. 81-84). Make a list of each of those responsibilities with a brief decription of each. Before the next election, make the effort to compare the candidates against that list. Find out how well they served in their past responsibilities. Remember, it is your responsibility as a Christian to try to select leaders who will be faithful to serve as ministers of God.

Scripture Index